EZEKIEL

Donald E. Gowan

KNOX PREACHING GUIDES

John H. Hayes, Editor

John Knox Press

ATLANTA

Library of Congress Cataloging in Publication Data

Gowan, Donald E.
    Ezekiel.

    (Knox preaching guides)
    1. Bible. O.T. Ezekiel—Criticism, interpretation, etc. I. Title. II. Series.
    BS1545.2.G68   1985   224'.406   84-48511
    ISBN 0-8042-3223-7 (pbk.)

© copyright John Knox Press 1985
10 9 8 7 6 5 4 3 2 1
Printed in the United States of America
John Knox Press
Atlanta, Georgia 30365

Contents

[Sequential Guide to passages on next page]

EZEKIEL

Introduction

The Prophet and His People

Ezekiel is not an easy book for the modern reader to appreciate. Its first chapter plunges us into a lengthy account of a bizarre visionary experience. Next we struggle through a series of stories about the peculiar behavior of the prophet, and then we are left stranded, it seems, in the morass of chapter after chapter of denunciations of the sins of Jerusalem and announcements of its inevitable fall. It is not a particularly attractive book, compared with Isaiah or Jeremiah. It requires some effort to learn to appreciate Ezekiel, but be assured the effort is worth expending, for this is an extremely important book. Ezekiel was a prophet to those Judeans who survived the fall of Jerusalem in 597 and 587 B.C., ministering to a few who found a way to continue as the people of Yahweh in exile. If they had not survived that greatest crisis in all of Israel's history there would have been no Judaism, no Christianity. It is the turning point from the ancient, national religion of Israel to the worldwide religion called Judaism which is marked by the book of Ezekiel. He is the last of the judgment prophets of the OT. The special message of that line of prophets beginning with Amos—that soon the old relationship between Yahweh and Israel would be brought to an end—was completely fulfilled within Ezekiel's lifetime. The questions he faced were, first, how to prepare the remnant of his people to deal with the end of all they had trusted in, and second, how to find a way to begin all over again.

In order to understand the message of this prophet, it is essential to know Ezekiel's congregation and the cataclysm they experienced, more important than knowing details about the life and personality of the prophet himself. Ezekiel keeps his own feelings and experiences very much in the background, but fortunately he does provide for us a series of clues about his audience, about the nature of their faith, their ethical standards, their hopes, and their despair. As we remind ourselves of the events this man and his people survived we may begin to realize that the harshness of the man is an accurate reflection of the harshness of the time in which he lived, and that the bizarre nature of parts of the book is in keeping with the bizarre experiences which his people had survived.

His book is carefully dated, so we know that Ezekiel's work as a prophet began in 592 B.C. and that he remained active until 571 among the Judeans who had been exiled to Babylonia. This enables us to establish the physical, emotional, and spiritual setting for the words of the book. Judah had been a vassal state, under the control of the new world-ruler, Nebuchadnezzar, from 605 to 597. (Details of the history of the period will not be offered here, as they are readily available in the standard histories of Israel, but note 2 Kings 24—25 and Jer 29, 39, 52 for biblical evidence of the time.) In 598/7 Jehoiakim, the vassal king, rebelled; Nebuchadnezzar and his armies appeared in Palestine, laid seige to Jerusalem, captured the city, looted it, and took the skilled workers and upper classes into exile. Jehoiakim conveniently died at that point and his successor, Jehoiachin, was exiled. 2 Kings 24:10–17 provides a few details:

> The king of Babylon ... carried off all the treasures of the house of the Lord, and the treasures of the king's house, and cut in pieces all the vessels of gold in the temple of the Lord, which Solomon king of Israel had made, as the Lord had foretold. He carried away all Jerusalem, and all the princes, and all the mighty men of valor, ten thousand captives, and all the craftsmen and the smiths; none remained, except the poorest people of the land (vss. 12–14).

The statement must not be taken too literally; members of the royal house still remained, for Zedekiah became the new vassal king and had officials serving him. Jeremiah the prophet and Baruch the scribe remained in Jerusalem, so the deportation was selective and not as wholesale as the words first lead us to think. Ezekiel must have been one of those taken away.

Let us not simply repeat the words without trying to understand what it does to a human being to go through such an experience. Jerusalem was a small city, by our standards, which means that one would know most of the people who died during those months. Ezekiel and those who would one day become his "congregation" knew what it was like to be bottled up inside a walled city with an enemy army camped outside. They had participated in caring for people wounded in the early fighting and had seen them die, had seen the food supplies becoming smaller, and had experienced hunger. Then the walls were breached; there was wholesale dying, fire, flight, rape, looting, terror, and grief. Families were separated, some people escaped, some just disappeared, many lay dead with no one to grieve for them or care for their bodies. In a few days, the survivors were rounded up and herded into refugee camps and marched away. Some families had succeeded in staying together, but many were now isolated individuals, still in shock from seeing their loved ones die, or frantic with anxiety because they did not know what had become of husband or child, wife or parent. And they walked, day after day, for weeks or months. The route from Palestine to Babylonia is about 900 miles. They walked, and more died, and they found themselves in a strange and forbidding land, not hilly and wooded like Palestine, but almost perfectly flat, marked only by great rivers and an extensive network of canals watering fertile fields; and here and there what seemed to them to be immense walled cities with temple towers looming into the heavens.

At the site of an old, ruined city, Tel Aviv, Ezekiel and some of the exiles were told they had come to their new home. It appears the Babylonians used such deported peoples to resettle deserted areas in order to improve the economy. One day, in that alien place, Ezekiel encountered afresh the God of Israel.

He was a member of a priestly family but in that foreign country it is doubtful that there were any priestly functions he would have believed it was legitimate to perform. But now he was called to be a prophet. He clearly stands in the line of OT judgment prophecy, but in many respects he differs from his predecessors, and for obvious reasons. Judgment is no longer future but has become present tense, for one thing, and before his ministry is ended judgment will have been completed. He works among those who have already been judged, and thus we find him functioning in a peculiarly pastoral way, as compared with the other prophets. His task was to keep the Yahwistic faith alive in a time of turmoil, suffering, and sorrow, when everything but mere existence had been lost, as daunting a task as anyone called to serve God has ever faced. On the human level, leaving the power of God out of it for the moment, let us estimate what his chances were. People are fond of speaking about the "faithful remnant" which survived the fall of Jerusalem and the exile. Let us see if we can locate such a faithful group with which Ezekiel might have worked.

If we search the prophetic and historical books of the OT for evidence of some group of people who actually believed Amos or Isaiah or Jeremiah, took their words seriously, changed their ways, and became the nucleus of a "faithful remnant," we search in vain. Those prophets failed, if their intended mission was to produce a well-disciplined group of people who fully understood the Yahwistic faith and were committed to keeping it. If we could locate such a group, and could trace some of them into exile, then we might be able to calculate, on the human level the prospect of the survival of Yahwism. But the book of Ezekiel tells us no such people existed (2:3–4; 3:7–9; 8:17–18). Certainly, pre-exilic Israel worshiped Yahweh, the God of the Exodus who had given them the Promised Land, celebrated Passover and brought him their offerings, and just as certainly they also worshiped Baal and Anat and Ashtoreth and Tammuz and who knows how many other gods. The prophetic books and the historical books make it clear that the practical monotheism of the Mosaic religion never took, was understood only by a very few, and nothing the prophets and reforming kings could do made any significant change. As we shall see, the events of the years just preceding Ezekiel's call hadn't made things any better. It is a defeated, demoralized, undisciplined group to which he is sent, the remnants of a people who had lost everything, and where their religion is concerned it becomes clear they didn't have much to begin with.

There was a community of sorts at Tel Aviv, by the River Chebar; Judeans transplanted to Babylonia, with a prophet living in their midst. But what future did they have? Was there any likelihood that they could maintain an identity which could preserve the uniqueness of the Yahwistic faith? How could we expect it, when even in their homeland, where tradition and culture and language and government and custom were all on the side of maintaining the ancestral faith, the essence of that faith had remained constantly in jeopardy and as practiced it was a mishmash of elements drawn from Yahwism, Canaanite religion, and who knows what else? Any judgment of their future, based on purely human factors, would have to expect them to assimilate to the predominant Babylonian culture within a few years, leaving nothing but a few vague recollections of Yahweh and Israel.

But the Yahwistic faith did survive, there in exile, and it did more than survive. Within two generations a new people was born; out of the exile came Judaism, a faith which insists with every word it utters that there exists only one God and that God cannot be represented by anything in the created world, a faith which has dedicated itself to following that God by the keeping of his law. They solved their identity problem in exile, and came out of it understanding that one can be a Jew anywhere, and that what makes one a Jew is obeying God. In the post-exilic period it is not only the prophetic types, scholars, and saints who understand that and are committed to it; the uniqueness of this religion which never quite sank in, before the exile, is now understood and accepted by ordinary people, and they are committed enough to it that they will die for it. The time will come when they do die for it.

We don't know just how that happened, but we know it did happen. There are no records from exile, between Ezekiel and Second Isaiah, and by the time the latter prophet began to speak the victory had been won. But Ezekiel gives us at least the beginning of it all, the desperateness of the aftermath of Jerusalem's fall, insights into the emotions of a defeated people, and struggles with the agonizing questions of faith which arise when everything goes wrong. More than any other prophet Ezekiel's work was done in response to human problems which determined what kind of activity he needed to perform; it was governed by life situations around him, issues and questions which he had to find some way to answer. It was a new life situation and thus the forms and usually also the substance of the issues were new, so we find in this book the efforts of a man to work without precedents to guide him. Here we find a pastor who has to improvise, to find new words, new explanations, and to do new things because the old ways provide no adequate response to the dilemmas his people now have to face.

How Shall We Preach from Ezekiel?

What do these words for exiles have to say to modern Christians? Two general suggestions of approaches to preaching Ezekiel will be offered here, to be illustrated throughout the book, and a brief, personal note will conclude this introduction.

Suppose we must address a congregation which seems to have nothing in common with those sixth century Judeans. Will that leave us without anything which we can take from Ezekiel which will be relevant to them? The answer is that if we believe that ours is a historical religion we do have something to preach from words which are addressed to people very different from us in specific times and situations which we have never experienced. What happened in the Babylonian exile is part of our history of salvation, part of the story of how God brought a rebellious people through national death to resurrection as a congregation committed to obeying him with all their hearts. From the prophetic interpretation of what God was doing in the midst of that history we can learn how the God we worship operates, and we can preach the truth about God's intention for his people (ourselves included), his diagnosis of their and our condition, and the measures he takes to cure it. All this is based on the assumption that although historical and social circumstances change radically, there is a consistency in God which can be depended on, and a certain consistency in human nature as well.

But is exile necessarily a condition which is totally foreign to modern Christians? Certainly the idea is not likely to be a popular one in most congregations, but it may be argued that both socially and theologically it is relevant to Christian life in ways which have so far been largely ignored.

There is a strand of thought in Christian history, going all the way back to the NT, which thinks of exile as the essence of Christian existence on earth. The Letter of James is addressed, "To the twelve tribes in the Dispersion," and 1 Peter begins with the salutation, "To the exiles of the Dispersion." Hebrews not only speaks of Abraham and Sarah as "strangers and exiles on the earth" (11:13), but indicates that their hope for a permanent city is the same as the expectation of Christians (compare 11:13–16 with 13:14). Those brief references are expanded in the description of Christians found in the *Epistle of Diognetus* (about A.D. 150):

> For Christians are distinguished from the rest of men neither by country nor by language nor by customs. For nowhere do they dwell in cities of their own; they do not use any strange form of speech or practise a singular mode of life.... But while they dwell in both Greek and barbarian cities, each as his lot was cast, and follow the customs of the land in dress and food and other matters of living, they show forth the remarkable and admittedly strange order of their own citizenship. They live in fatherlands of their own, but as aliens. They share all things as citizens, and suffer all things as strangers. Every foreign land is their fatherland, and every fatherland a foreign land (5:1–2, 4–5).

Within a few centuries, however, Christianity became established and acculturated, and the concept of living as strangers and exiles in one's own homeland has appeared for the most part only among sectarian groups. There have been real, physical exiles enough in our history, and for those who have experienced those dislocations, forced or by choice, the exile materials in the OT have had an obvious relevance. But in our own time, among the established churches, there have been voices raised to suggest that it is appropriate for the church to consider itself to be living in exile, no matter where it is or what its status.

George W. Webber, in his book, *Today's Church: A Community of Exiles and Pilgrims*, writes, "I suggest that for Christians in an affluent world, in a nation as powerful and self-righteous as the United States, the only rational posture for us must also be one of aliens or exiles" (p. 12). He takes

the advice which Jeremiah wrote to the Babylonian exiles
(chap. 29) to be normative for Christian existence, reminding
us that we need to recognize that the Christian ethic and that
of the society in which we live are not the same, that we have
distinctive concerns and goals which are not shared by the
culture at large, and that nevertheless we are to "seek the
welfare of the city" (Jer 29:7) in which we live, even by serving as its critics, where necessary.

From a very different point of view, the Roman Catholic
theologian Karl Rahner, has taken up the question of "The
Teaching of Vatican II on the Church and the Future Reality
of Christian Life," but has reached some conclusions remark-
ably similar to those of Webber. As he projects what the future of Christianity may be like, he suggests:

> Everywhere they will be a little flock, because mankind
> grows quicker than Christendom and because men will not be
> Christians by custom and tradition, through institutions and
> history, or because of the homogeneity of a social milieu and
> public opinion, but—leaving out of account the sacred flame
> of parental example and the intimate sphere of home, family
> and small groups—they will be Christians only because of
> their own act of faith attained in a difficult struggle and per-
> petually achieved anew. Everywhere will be diaspora and the
> diaspora will be everywhere. . . . And since the Christians will
> form only a relatively small minority with no independent
> historical domain of existence of their own, they will all,
> though in varying degrees, live in the "diaspora of the Gen-
> tiles" (pp. 78–79).

Rahner does not see that potential future as anything to fear
or lament, but projects new possibilities of commitment and
mission for that church which is everywhere in exile. "It will
be dependent in everything on faith and on the holy power of
the heart, for it will no longer be able to draw any strength at
all, or very little, from what is purely institutional" (p. 80).

The insights of these writers into our present situation as
Christians in cultures which really do not support our ethos,
even though many of us still find it hard to accept that, may
help us to see how words addressed to exiles long ago can
enlighten our own self-understanding, provide encourage-
ment in the midst of confusing change, and challenge us to
find new ways to "seek the welfare of the city" in which we
sojourn.

There are many real exiles in our congregations—people
now living far from the place in which they grew up, not
knowing how long they will stay in their present location,
having a rootless feeling which gives them only weak motiva-
tions to commit themselves to the needs and potentials of
their present sojourning place. Preaching the exile materials
of the OT may speak to them with a peculiar directness, to
help them obtain a sense of stability in the midst of physical
rootlessness, and to enable them to accept responsibility for
what is in many ways someone else's world.

Preaching the exile message may also help those who too
comfortably associate Christianity with life as it always has
been to free themselves from bondage to their culture and to
find in their religion both a critique of the *status quo* and the
assurances that change need not be destructive.

Furthermore, reflection on the experiences of those Judean
exiles of long ago may remind us of the brothers and sisters
in Christ who are involuntary exiles in our own time, and in
daily need of support from those who have a place they can
call their own.

Now for the personal note. These pages have been influenced by contact with an exile experience of a peculiar sort.
For two years the author has been pulpit supply for a group
of people who have chosen to remain loyal to their denomi-
nation even though their former minister persuaded the majority of the congregation to withdraw and to attempt
(successfully so far) to claim the property for the dissident
group. The loyal people have found themselves to be a
church, without a building, but they *are* a church. My first
sermon to them was from Ezek 37 and when I called them a
congregation in exile, they found that Ezekiel was not so forbidding after all, but spoke rather directly to them about
things they understood. Some of what I have learned about
Ezekiel, then, I have learned from preaching to Christians in
exile, and this book is dedicated to those people.

For discussions of the critical questions concerning the
book of Ezekiel, it will be necessary to consult one of the excellent modern commentaries which are available. This book
is not intended to replace commentaries but to be a supplement to them, providing the kind of help for the preacher
which they usually do not offer—that is, how to make the

move from what the message meant to ancient Israel to a
preachable message for our own day. Some of the key critical
questions will of necessity be alluded to here and there, and
the position taken in this book will be stated without arguing
the case. The interpretation is based on the present scholarly
consensus that Ezekiel's ministry took place entirely in the
Babylonian exile (not in Palestine, or in both places), and
that most of the book is his work, although parts of it come
from his disciples. Much of the scholarship produced between 1920 and 1950 contained radical challenges to those
positions, but recent work has provided a secure critical
foundation on which the discussion of the prophet's theology
can be built. The conclusion that every part of the book reflects conditions in the Babylonian exile is essential to the
interpretation offered here, but questions of authorship are
less significant. The position taken here is that for preaching
purposes the difference between the original words of Ezekiel
and the additions of disciples is usually not important, for it
is the canonical, that is, the final, form of the book, that combination of the prophet's own words and the contributions of
those who first sought to understand him and apply his
words, which has become the word of God to the believing
community from the sixth century B.C. to the present.

Ezekiel is a carefully organized book, with chapters 1—24
dealing primarily with events between the prophet's call in
592 and the fall of Jerusalem in 587, chapters 25—32 present-
ing a series of oracles against foreign nations, and chapters
33—48 offering promises concerning the coming of a new
age. In the commentary which follows you will find a discussion of each section of the book, usually in the original, scrip-
tural order, but in order to provide the fullest possible
discussion of some of the special features of Ezekiel's work,
certain related passages have been grouped (for example, all
the allegories are discussed in one place), but cross-referenc-
ing should make it easy to locate the discussion of each
passage.

A Prophet to the Exiles:
Ezekiel's Call
(Ezekiel 1:1—3:15)

The first chapter of Ezekiel is probably as difficult for the preacher as any part of the book, but it is not impossible, by any means. Let us approach it in this way: If this is God's revelation to his people, as we assume it to be, then it must be a divine response to some human need, for there is no indication that God bothers to reveal to us things we don't really need to know. What then is the problem which calls forth such a response as this?

The Situation

Something of the physical and spiritual circumstances of the exiles in Babylonia has already been sketched in the introduction, but there is a theological issue which needs to be outlined here. Every nation in antiquity tended to associate its deities with its own territory, and Israel was no exception, even though already in the Exodus story they had evidence that theirs was a God who might make his power felt in a land which presumably belonged to other gods. So just as Naaman the Syrian assumed that in order to worship Yahweh in his homeland he would have to have two mules' burdens of earth from Yahweh's land on which to build an altar (2 Kings 5:17), David also lamented the prospect of being driven "away from the presence of the Lord" (1 Sam 26:19-20). That attitude had not changed by the time of the fall of Jerusalem, as the psalm of the exiles reveals: "How shall we sing the Lord's song in a foreign land?" (Ps 137:4). Now Ezekiel and his people find themselves in an "unclean land" (Amos 7:17), separated from access to the temple in Jerusalem or any of the traditional sanctuaries where Yahweh made himself known. The first problem to which the vision is a response, then, is the question of access to God.

A second theological issue created by the fall of Jerusalem struck even more deeply, if possible, at the heart of the people's faith, and that was the question of whether any satisfac-

tory explanation could be offered for the disasters which had
befallen the nation chosen to be his own and the land and
city chosen to be his dwelling place. One possible explanation was that the gods of Babylon had demonstrated their
superiority to Yahweh, the Israelite god, via the superiority
of Nebuchadnezzar's armies to the armies of Judah. Another
was that Yahweh had simply abandoned his people and no
longer intended to keep any of his promises. That both ideas
were circulating among the exiles becomes evident from the
emphases of Ezekiel's teaching, and his inaugural vision is
already a response to both.

The Meaning of the Prophetic Call

God's initial response to the dilemmas created by exile was
to commission a man to be his prophet. Even in Babylonia
they were not to be left without a word from the Lord who
had claimed them as his own. The call to be a prophet in a
foreign land does have some earlier parallels, both connected
with Sinai. Before Israel existed as a nation and had a land of
its own Yahweh encountered Moses at Horeb (Sinai), speaking to him from a burning bush to commission him to lead
his people out of slavery (Exod 3). Centuries later, Elijah was
recommissioned at Horeb, after experiencing wind, earthquake, and fire (1 Kings 19). But even though Sinai was
outside the Promised Land proper it was known to be the
Mountain of God, and so there is something novel about
Ezekiel's experience. With the exception of the call of Moses,
it is the most lengthy and detailed of the Bible's call stories.
There was a traditional pattern by which one spoke in Israel
of having received such a commission from God, and the
parts of the standard form can be found in chapters 1—3. If
you are focusing on the call experience in your interpretation
of this section, it will be helpful to compare Ezekiel with
Moses (Exod 3—6), Gideon (Judges 6), Samuel (1 Sam 3),
Isaiah (Isa 6), Jeremiah (Jer 1:4–10), and for aspects of the
visionary experience 1 Kings 22 and Daniel 10 are also instructive. (Paul's vision should also be compared, Acts 9:3–9;
22:6–11; 26:12–18). The call story begins with an encounter
of a human being with God, sometimes described very
briefly and elsewhere in great detail. The commission is typically the second element, and that is normally followed by a

negative reaction on the part of the human being, who feels overwhelmed by the task assigned, and the final element is usually the divine assurance that the resources necessary to do the job will be provided. As you compare these stories you will see that several variations of the pattern are possible, but that the relationships among them are clear.

Now, why were these call stories recorded? Just because they were sensational experiences? It seems likely that there was a sounder reason than that. Each of the individuals named made strong claims to authority which had no institutional backing. They asserted an authority which they believed had been given them directly by God, and it is likely that the call story was their response to questions like, "Who put you in charge?" But that is no issue for us; those who accept the essential truth of the Scriptures are not likely to question the authority of Moses or Ezekiel today. What, then, does the call story have to say to us? Caution is necessary here, for not everyone is called by God to do a work analogous to that of Moses or Ezekiel, so these are not stories which can be said to apply to everybody. Some people are indeed called to special tasks in our day, but not to be prophets in the sense that Isaiah or Ezekiel were—at least anyone who claims to have the authority to be able to announce exactly what God is doing in our time is making a very audacious claim!

The form of the call story, nonetheless, reveals some profound truths about ourselves and the way God works with us. Notice that the people he chooses never seem very well qualified for the work he assigns them. And they know it. But God makes it clear that he has his own reasons for choosing people whom human wisdom would exclude, and these stories suggest that it may well be that it is those who know how poorly qualified they are whom God can use most effectively. At any rate, the call story always makes it clear that when God chooses a person to do a job he also provides whatever resources are needed in order to get it done. Now in Ezekiel's case, the effect of the vision is so overpowering that he is unable to argue or protest, as Gideon or Jeremiah do, he just keels over and requires divine help even to get back on his feet. But with the other call stories as background, the meaning of all the warnings to be faithful and reassurances of strength to meet the challenge in chapters 2 and 3 fall into place as parts of a familiar pattern. Because what is said to Ezekiel is not unique, then, but reaffirms what the Bible regularly has to say about how God calls ordinary people to do his work, it seems legitimate to believe that we who receive lesser calls may also expect the same kind of help. (For the distinctive elements of Ezekiel's commission, see Section 2— The Watchman.)

The Details of the Vision

There is no end to the difficulties involved in trying to comprehend what Ezekiel actually saw by the River Chebar that day. The Hebrew text itself seems to have been very poorly transmitted, for some verses are almost untranslatable, and every English version is an improvement on the Hebrew (which is to say, the translators are guessing). The parts which read clearly are astonishing enough. You must consult the commentaries for a verse-by-verse discussion of the vision; here you will find an interpretation of why he saw what he did, and of what that meant to him and can mean to us. Here is a case where the discoveries of the past 200 years in the Middle East can be of help to the Bible interpreter. Careful studies of the art of the region have located parallels to almost every feature described by Ezekiel; in other words his vision, like the experiences of visionaries in other cultures, was described by him in terms of images drawn from the culture he knew. Creatures with four wings and multiple faces, representations of deities enthroned above animals of one kind or another and wheeled thrones may be found represented in a great variety of ways in the art of the ancient Near East. Let us see if we can imagine why people of the past created such figures—surely they had not seen such things! Having said that, we are probably on the way to an answer. They were trying to represent visually their convictions about an unseen world, the world of gods and genies and demons and spirits of various kinds. To do that they used elements from the visible world and combined them in ways which never occur in nature so as to depict another kind of reality. In Mesopotamia, Ezekiel would have been in the presence of such imagery almost daily, and just as our inner experiences are shaped by what we see and know in the world around us, so Ezekiel's comprehension of what happened to him that day was aided by what he had seen of efforts to represent visually an otherwise unknowable aspect of reality.

How much actual description does he give us? That is an important question, lest we get off on the wrong foot. It was ignoring the fact that the whole vision reflects the culture of the day and ignoring the fact that the prophet makes no attempt to tell us what anything *really* looked like that led to the bizarre modern effort to reconstruct the throne chariot of God as a space ship. Notice how many times the prophet uses the words "likeness," "appearance," "like." The apparently odd combination of confused language and careful qualification of what is said should reveal to us that the prophet is very well aware that he cannot describe what he has experienced. This is an effort to describe the indescribable, namely the sense of knowing that God himself is very immediately present. The carefulness of his choice of words is demonstrated when he at last indicates to us that in fact it is God who is enthroned above that fantastic chariot: "Such was the *appearance* of the *likeness* of the *glory* of the Lord" (1:28). He makes sure that he is three steps removed from saying anything about what God looks like!

But God was there, in some special manifestation which knocked Ezekiel flat. And we can begin to see why the details of the vision are of some importance, difficult though they may be, and foreign to the experiences of many of us. (This author is not a visionary, but acknowledges that there are authentic visionaries in our midst who understand some of this better than he does.) The prophet uses imagery drawn from the attempts of people around him to represent an unseen world, which is real, though invisible in order to say to us that he encountered a reality there by the River Chebar which is so different from anything we know in this world that ordinary language is completely inadequate to represent it. He had to do something creative with language, and the imagery of the culture of the ancient Near East helped him to do it. The throne chariot (only a throne, take note, not an effort to depict the deity, as the other cultures did try to do), appears in the midst of more traditional representations of the presence of God, which we call "theophany" in OT study.

This is the storm (1:4), with emphasis on wind and fire. The experiences of Moses and Elijah at Sinai were mentioned earlier, and now you might recall Exod 19 and its classical description of theophany in the OT. In theophanies the most powerful and awe-inspiring aspects of nature—storms and earthquakes (possibly also volcanic eruptions and in some texts, floods)— are brought together to express how people *feel* when they know that God in all his power is that near to them. Ezekiel's combination of the throne-chariot with the traditional language of theophany serves to intensify even more the impression of terrifying energy which he encountered. Notice the continual and completely untrammeled movement of the chariot itself and of the flashing lights within it.

There is a major theme of the book of Ezekiel which appears with unparalleled intensity in this first section and which may be expressed in words spoken to another prophet long before: "I am God and not man, the Holy One in your midst" (Hos 11:9). The energy, awesomeness, otherworldliness, and essential indescribability of the vision is one way of expressing that absolute difference. Another way, which appears as a reminder throughout the book, is the term "son of man," by which God always addresses Ezekiel. It is a regular reminder of his humanity over against that wholly other Reality which he encountered at the river, and so the TEV rendition "mortal man" is a fairly appropriate translation. If it were not for the science fiction overtones carried by "earthling," that would be even more appropriate.

What does it all mean? It is a way of expressing Ezekiel's conviction that he had encountered something very real, very powerful but totally different from anything one can describe in this world. This is that "Wholly Other" we talk about. God in himself cannot begin to be described but he can be encountered, and the encounter leaves one with an awesome sense of incredible energy and of the absolute difference between oneself and God. Do such encounters really happen? Yes, they do. But of what use are such outlandish descriptions to the rest of us earthbound folk who have never felt or seen any such thing? The answer is, we are the ones who need this, because without such reminders of what God is really like, we are likely to create tame and good-mannered deities in our own stodgy likeness. One theme which can be and sometimes needs to be preached from this aspect of Ezekiel's vision was summed up by J. B. Phillips in several chapters of his book *Your God Is Too Small*. These are the unreal gods in his book which are demolished by the God who appeared to Ezekiel: Grand Old Man, Meek-and-Mild, Heavenly Bosom, Pale Galilean, and especially God-in-a-Box. When those idols are detected lurking in the corners of your church, it may be possible to find a way to let Ezekiel speak to them.

The Implications of the Vision

God commissioned a prophet that day to offer to his people an explanation of what it really meant that Jerusalem had fallen and would fall again. We shall deal with that explanation and the further consequences of the fall at great length in what follows, but something more needs to be said about the implicit message conveyed by the occurrence of the vision itself. Jerusalem is supposed to be Yahweh's throne, the place he has chosen to make his name to dwell and Canaan is the land he chose to make a home for his people. But now, far away from the Promised Land and that temple, in an unclean land, Yahweh appears in all his power and glory. That priest whose exile made it impossible to serve God is offered a new way to serve. It is a long commissioning speech, most of chapters 2 and 3, but in it he is not told what he will have to say or do, just that he must speak what God gives him to say. He is warned that he will face a hostile audience, that his words will be unpleasant and his task a thankless one, but he is assured that God will be with him to bring him through it. And even in the midst of all those negative words there is a surprising message of good news. For God is there, in exile, speaking to one of his supposedly repudiated people and promising to speak through him to all the exiles. They are not lost, God has not abandoned them, he is not confined to that temple where they had thought they had to go to find him. God is free, alive and active with overwhelming power, and he comes to them. A great deal more needed to be said, but without the assurance of the truth of that first word, none of it could be believed, and that first word is: God is here.

That original message is certainly not for us. We do not

think God is confined to Jerusalem. An essential feature of
Christian teaching is that God is accessible anywhere, but
one thing we learn from Ezekiel about our own faith is how
our ancestors in the faith came to know that is true. And have
we learned the lesson thoroughly enough that we do not at
times attempt to confine God to certain buildings, certain de-
nominations or nations, certain formulas which define what
he can and cannot do? God is free, and that can be as terrifying now as the vision was to Ezekiel. Sometimes, if you
dare, that needs to be preached.

The Meaning of the Commission

Not an attractive congregation, the one to which Ezekiel is
sent! "Son of man, I send you to the people of Israel, to a
nation of rebels, who have rebelled against me; they and
their fathers have transgressed against me to this very day.
The people also are impudent and stubborn . . ." (2:3–4). But
this also is a familiar part of the call of a prophet. Jeremiah
was told, of his audience, "Be not afraid of them, for I am
with you to deliver you" (1:8), and he learned to his great
distress that to speak the words of a prophet was to produce
hatred and even threats on his life (see 11:18–23). Instead of
opposition, it is the utter hopelessness of the people to whom
Isaiah had to speak which is emphasized in his commission:
"Hear and hear, but do not understand, see and see, but do
not perceive" (6:9). That message given to Isaiah has been a
problem to many interpreters of the prophets because they
have come to these books with the preconceived idea that the
prophets were preachers of repentance who came to offer
their people a chance to reform before it was too late. But
Isaiah is told it is already too late, and a very careful reading
of the OT prophetic books shows that in fact they very rarely
called for repentance with any accompanying promise that a
changed life would bring a changed future. Their essential
message is that Israel has perennially refused to repent, for
so long that at last their sins have found them out and now
judgment is at hand. To put it crudely, the old plan has not
worked, and now God is about to start all over.

No wonder the prophets encountered such fierce opposition, if that was their essential message! But the truth of
their words was finally becoming evident to Ezekiel and his

people; Jerusalem did fall to Nebuchadnezzar and the exiles had lost everything. But as we shall soon see, they insist on pinning their last hopes on something which other prophets had already attacked as invalid: the idea that the temple is invulnerable. Ezekiel will boldly assert that Jerusalem and its temple will soon be no more, and that heresy will put him in danger of his very life. So he is warned from the beginning that the rebellions of Israel are not only a part of all her past history, but will be encountered by him in person among the exiles. He, like the others, will find that to be a prophet means to have to bear suffering and disgrace. Thus, he will be given a tough armor, and seldom will we ever be permitted to see the man behind it, although here and there he will reveal a glimpse of his feelings. Since he is living through the turning point in God's work with his people, Ezekiel's ministry will, toward the end, become different from his predecessors. His office as a watchman and his preaching of the possibility of repentance in chapter 18 represent the beginning of the new age. But his message prior to the fall of Jerusalem in 587 B.C. is the same as the other judgment prophets: God has given his people covenant, law, king, priest, and land, but they have continually disobeyed him and have so adamantly refused to become the people defined by his covenant that he has now determined to bring all that to an end, and start over.

This has crucial implications for our preaching of the prophets. It means that their message was a completely time-conditioned one, not valid for all people and every time, but a message dealing quite specifically with what was going to happen to Israel in the eighth century and to Judah early in the sixth. We are not homiletically justified in taking their words and simply transferring them to contemporary situations, unless one of us has received new divine insight that the end is now also at hand for the church!

So what is there to preach from the judgment messages of prophets from Amos through Ezekiel? The answer is that primarily the message is theological rather than ethical, but the ethical implications are also present, and with considerable power. It is premature to begin to develop that theology in connection with this section of the book (the classical statement of it does not appear until chap. 37), but in essence we are dealing with the prophetic understanding of how God works through the history of a people, to guide and to instruct, and also if need be to destroy and re-create, as he works toward the salvation of humanity. It is the desperateness of the human condition and the unchangeable determination of God to accomplish his will which is the heart of the prophetic word. There is something of the theology of the cross in all of that. The ethical side of the message, for us, is this: Israel had its chance, and muffed it. When Amos began to speak God had already determined upon a new way, but maybe it is not too late for us, for the church. And if there is still time for us to be a people after God's own heart, then we need to hear the prophetic definition of God's standards with the utmost seriousness (as eventually the exiles in Babylonia did) and to do them with great enthusiasm—not in order to avoid disaster, but to show that we can become that people of God which he has been at work to create through this history to which Ezekiel contributed, this history of Israel, of Judaism, of Jesus of Nazareth, and of the Church.

The Watchman
(Ezekiel 3:16–21; 33:1–9)

The impact of the vision of the throne chariot upon Ezekiel was so profound that he returned to his home among the exiles at Tel Aviv and "sat there overwhelmed among them seven days" (3:15). Then, we are told, he received a second commission, to be a watchman responsible for the destiny of each individual among his people. This section has a parallel later in the book (3:16b–19 is almost identical to 33:7–9), and as the two passages are compared it seems very likely that 3:16–21 is out of order chronologically. For the most part, Ezekiel is a much more carefully ordered book than the earlier prophetic books, with many dated chapters, but even the dates are not in perfect order, where a topical arrangement seemed more important (compare 29:1, 17, and 31:1), so we need not assume that the present arrangement of the book follows the chronology of the prophet's career exactly. Chapters 1—24 mostly come from before the fall of Jerusalem in 587, the oracles against the nations in 25—32 are dated between 587 and 585, and most of chapters 33—48 come from after 587. Chapter 33, which also contains a watchman passage, thus represents the turning point in Ezekiel's work, from prophecy of judgment to promise of restoration and his special commission seems to fit the beginning of that new era better than it does the time before Jerusalem's fall. It is generally believed, then, that when the book was edited into its final form it was thought appropriate to add an exerpt from that watchman passage as a supplement to Ezekiel's original call in order to provide at the beginning a more complete picture of the nature of his ministry. This brief summary of critical conclusions will explain why both texts are being discussed here, but with reference to a post-587 situation.

Here we encounter our first evidence of Ezekiel's role as a pastor. The traditional prophetic role of messenger, sent to announce the word of God to Israel, has now been supplemented with a ministry to individuals. (For more on the "individualism" of Ezekiel, see section 8, on chap. 18.) The work of a watchman in wartime (we would say a person on guard-duty), is described in what seems unnecessary detail in 33:1–6, for these people had just been through a war and would understand all that very well. The one aspect of the description which is relevant to Ezekiel's work is *responsibility* for the welfare of others. He must do more than simply announce the word of God to the congregation; in the new situation after 587, when God is beginning to create his people of the new covenant, it now becomes a matter of individual choice, on the part of each one of the exiles, whether to give up and just assimilate to the predominant Babylonian culture, or to try to find a way to preserve identity and integrity as members of the people of Yahweh. And it is Ezekiel's responsibility to put the challenge to each person, not to let one of his people slip away without being confronted with a warning about the significance of his choice. (As for the meaning of "wicked," "righteous," "life," and "death," see the comments on chap. 18.)

Before 587 the prophetic message had been concerned with the destiny of the nation, and as the concluding part of section 1 indicated, the prophets were under the conviction that its destiny was settled; it was too late to change. After 587, there is no nation left, and it seems to have been a major part of Ezekiel's work to attempt to create a faithful community, person by person, calling for individual decisions.

It has been observed that as a parable, the story of the watchman in 33:1–6 does not fit Ezekiel's work very exactly, for the watchman is appointed by the people to warn them of the coming of the enemy. But Yahweh appoints Ezekiel, and in the language of the parable, Yahweh is also the enemy. Two comments need to be made on that. If we accept the conclusions of NT scholars about parables, that they are stories intended to make only one point, then we can see that the point of the watchman story is responsibility for the fate of one's people, and that carries over perfectly to Ezekiel's commission. But in fact there is some truth also in the tension between the details of the story and the prophet's role, for that reflects a tension in God's revelation of how he works with us. It is God who judges, in his justice, but it is not God's ultimate intention to judge, but to give life (more on this in section 8). So in fact it is true that it is the "enemy" who appoints the watchman, and we see that the apparent inappropriateness of the story is in fact a pointer to a profound truth about the nature of our God, and a pointer to the message of the NT.

These passages may be preached, then, for what they tell us of a God who at the same time upholds justice and righteousness *and* desires only life for his people. Or, perhaps more appropriately, the human side of the matter may be emphasized, and that is the placing of responsibility for the life of every member of his congregation on Ezekiel's shoulders. It is not enough for him to stand before them and speak the truth, he must also put the necessity for decision personally to each one of them and must warn any of them who are tempted to slip away of the consequences of such a choice. Who could bear such a responsibility? Who could be so intimately involved in the lives of other people? Surely the role of watchman is not one we covet for ourselves or will inflict upon the members of our congregations wholesale, as if every Christian bore the same measure of responsibility as Ezekiel! For he was a prophet, a man of God of a unique kind, and as we shall see in the next section, he was asked to carry a burden which God imposes upon only a few. All the institutions of his religion had been destroyed and there remained only a thoroughly demoralized people in that day. Humanly speaking, as far as we can see, the future depended on Ezekiel's faithfulness. Note that, under those circumstances, the warnings he was impelled to offer actually contained within them an element of good news, for the warning to avoid the ways of death implies that life is still possible. We shall see that after 587 that was not an easy message to believe.

Ezekiel's role in that time of crisis does remind us that similar responsibilities do fall upon one person or one small group of people in other crisis situations, and we have seen that the essence of the prophet's responsibility was to make sure that the possibility of new life was not lost to anyone. On first reading about his function as a watchman it seems that he was commissioned to be a kind of moral policeman, with the duty to check up on everyone's behavior—hardly an attractive role to most of us, not least because we know of some Christian leaders who have tried to do that, with unfortunate results. We don't know how Ezekiel carried out his responsibility, but the interpretation offered here has emphasized it as a pastoral role, taking seriously the welfare of each individual under his care, rather than that of policeman. And the need to care for individuals is not confined to those called to be prophets.

Living the Message:
Symbolic Acts
(Ezekiel 3:22—5:17; 12:1–20; 24:15–27)

After the report of Ezekiel's call, the behavior of the prophet is said to have been profoundly affected by his commission, for a series of short narratives tells of the ways in which he not only spoke but also acted out his message. Symbolic acts appear occasionally in stories about earlier prophets (see 1 Kings 11: 29–39; Hos 3; Isa 20), but they come to special prominence in Jeremiah and his younger contemporary Ezekiel. More are recorded for Ezekiel than for any other prophet, and he is the last prophet in the OT who is said to have behaved in this way. Since the symbolic acts tell us something about the nature of prophecy itself, the most important of those ascribed to Ezekiel will be discussed together in this section, even though some of them are found later in the book.

Several explanations of the meaning of the symbolic acts have been offered. Some of them we need not concern ourselves with, for they do not fit the evidence very well; for example, the claim that they are something like parables, spoken but not really acted out, the effort to account for them as involuntary reactions to the state of ecstasy, and the theory that they are symptoms of psychosis. But this leaves two explanations to consider, (1) the interpretation of them as just illustrations of the message (we probably would call them object lessons), as ways of getting people's attention, and (2) the theory that they were actually effective actions, with something like a magical power to bring to pass what was being performed. If the divine *word* was believed to be effective, once uttered (see Isa 55:10–11), so also they might have thought the symbolic acts of the prophets to be another means by which God could accomplish his will. We shall consider these two options along the way, and will add to them an additional interpretation based on the fact that some of the symbolic acts had profound effects on the life of the man who performed them. After each passage has been discussed in turn the section will be concluded by some reflections about what symbolic acts reveal to us concerning the office of prophet, for that is probably the most important aspect of these texts for preaching. The message conveyed to the exiles by these acts was the same as Ezekiel pronounced elsewhere in more straightforward ways, namely that the fall of Jerusalem was imminent. But the life of the prophet also became a message of another kind to the descendents of the exiles and we can see in it a pointer toward the NT.

The Prophet's Inability to Speak (3:22–27)

This is a difficult passage to understand and it is not certain that it should even be called a symbolic act, but it is included here because of its similarity to chapter 4 and because it provides additional information on how the prophetic office affected the life of the one called to it. In another vision of the glory of the Lord, which occurred some time after his inaugural vision, Ezekiel is told to shut himself up within his house and learns that then he will be bound with cords and will be unable to speak. But after this come many chapters of speeches and public actions. Here it is said he will be "dumb and unable to reprove them" (3:26), but the book is full of reproofs. It has been suggested that here we have another example of something which happened to him around the time of the fall of Jerusalem which has been inserted early in the book, as the watchman passage was, for the promise that Ezekiel will no longer be dumb appears in association with the death of his wife, in 24:25– 27, and the fulfillment of that is recorded in 33:21–22. It may be, then, that the period of dumbness did not extend from his call in 592 through 585, but from the time he became aware that Jerusalem had fallen, in 587, through the receipt of the message in 585. If so, we might understand his remaining at home, silent and virtually motionless as an appropriate participation in the terrible calamity that had just befallen his people. But if the passage must be dated at the very beginning of his ministry, its meaning is much more difficult to ascertain.

The Seige of Jerusalem (4:1–3)

This is either a kind of object lesson, to attempt to force the exiles to think about the possibility that Jerusalem might have to undergo another seige, or it was thought to be an effective action, considering Ezekiel's little model city surrounded by seigeworks to be an act which would trigger the real event. Note that he is to set his face toward the city, that is to play the role of the enemy, and ultimately the enemy, the one who has determined that this shall be, is God. In the symbolic acts, sometimes the prophet is called upon to stand for God and sometimes for the people, and in the conclusion to this section we shall want to draw some conclusions about the significance of that. The Hebrew term for what we are calling symbolic act is "sign," as can be seen in vs. 3.

Bearing Their Iniquity (4:4–8)

Ezekiel is ordered to lie down upon his left side for 390 days (according to the Hebrew text; the Greek text has 190 days, which many scholars think is more likely to be original), then to turn over and lie on his right side for 40 days. Now the prophet represents not God as he did in 4:1–3 but the people, and what he does is a feeble sort of object lesson or effective act. Something else seems to be happening, and it is explained for us. "I will lay the punishment of the house of Israel upon you" (vs. 4); ". . . and bear the punishment of the house of Judah" (vs. 6). Lying on his side, virtually motionless (vs. 8), does not really act out anything that will happen to others, unless it is a kind of symbolic death, but as we begin to visualize it, and feel it, we can realize the physical distress and the humiliation it caused the prophet. Only that makes the statement that he will "bear the punishment" understandable. Questions have been raised about whether this is physically possible, assuming that he didn't move at all for the entire period, and one answer that has been offered is the suggestion that he was in a catatonic state. But we should not get sidetracked by issues of that kind, for very little is said about exactly what he did. For all we know he may have left home in the morning, lay down on his left side in the market place for all to see him, and at night got up and gone home. He must have been in a public place, at any rate, and we can at least imagine what it would have been like, lying in the dust day after day, listening to the kinds of comments that would be likely to come from those who looked down at him. What do we encounter in this symbolic act but a suffer-

ing servant of the Lord? We begin to learn that to be a
prophet means not only to announce the will of God, to stand
on God's side, over against the people if need be, but also to
live the will of God, even when that involves the judgment of
a rebellious people. The number of days which he must lie on
his side is said to represent the number of years of their punishment. Older commentators took this to be a reference to
the history of Israel's rebellion, looking backward after it had
happened. The opinions of recent commentaries consider the
numbers to be predictions of the length of the exile. The last
seems to provide a superior explanation. This is the only
place in which the role of the prophet in a symbolic act is
given such an explicit interpretation (as in vs. 4), so despite
the obscurities of the text it must be considered a very important one.

Seige Rations (4:9–17)

Ezekiel's sufferings and their relationship to what would actually be happening very soon to his people in Jerusalem are
more obvious in this symbolic act. He is to make bread from an
odd mixture of grains, just as those under seige will have to eat
anything they can get their hands on, and he must strictly limit
the amount he eats and drinks. Each commentator has a
slightly different estimate of the measures, but there is general
agreement that he had about a half-pound of bread a day and
most think the one-sixth hin would have been a little less than
a quart of water, so he must subsist on poor and very scanty
rations. Furthermore, since in a Middle Eastern city under
seige, wood for cooking fires would probably be in short supply, he is to bake his bread on a fire made of dried human dung.
At this point we encounter the only serious protest Ezekiel ever
made. He was a priest and had carefully observed the laws of
ritual cleanness all his life. No doubt there had been necessary
exceptions during the seige and the march to Babylonia, but he
had never deliberately defiled himself, and now God is in-
structing him to do just that! And, to Ezekiel's one protest God
does respond, allowing him to use a more common fuel of that
region, dried animal dung.

This kind of behavior involves the entire life of the prophet
too deeply to be appropriately called an illustration of his
message or an object lesson. Also, to say that his activities

triggered the historical event hardly does justice to what was happening to the man Ezekiel. It is becoming clear from this sequence of symbolic acts that to be a prophet required him to participate to the fullest possible extent in the life of his people, those people who stood under judgment. If intense suffering was to be their lot, then it must also be the lot of God's prophet.

Shaving and Destroying (5:1–17)

In a solemn absurdity, Ezekiel now used a sword (cf. chap. 21 which is a series of oracles connected by the leitmotif "sword"), to shave off his hair and beard, then carefully goes through a strange bit of play-acting. He uses balances to divide it into three equal parts (weighing probably already signifies judging, as it clearly did later on, see Dan 5:27), then burns one part, strikes another with the sword, and throws the third part into the wind. A small amount of the hair he saves, binding it up in the hem of his robe, but then takes even some of that and burns it also. Why hair should be used to represent the people of Israel is not at all obvious, but there are references to shaving elsewhere which help us to understand the reason for the first part of the act. It might have been seen as an appropriate prophetic response to the message which he was compelled to give concerning the impending fall of Jerusalem, for shaving the hair and beard was practiced at times as a sign of mourning (see Jer 41:5; 48:37). Since the forceable shaving of someone was considered an extreme humiliation (2 Sam 10:4–5; Isa 7:20), Ezekiel may also have understood his experience to be a sharing of the indignities which the people of Jerusalem would soon have to endure. But then the hair is used to represent the fate of those people as he acts out a message which will be delivered orally many additional times: Some will die by fire and some by sword, and those who are left alive will be scattered among the nations.

No symbolic act was intended to be cryptic. The meaning of many of them was obvious and needed no interpretation, but in other cases Ezekiel explains himself, as he does in 5:5–17, most of which refers to the symbolic use of the hair, but some of which may also allude to the other acts recorded in chapter 4. The nature of the message and questions about what can be preached from it today will be discussed more fully in the next section, but some of the special emphases of the chapter should be mentioned here. The unique character of Jerusalem, which Ezekiel's people were depending on to save it from every enemy, is emphasized here in thoroughly negative ways. That Jerusalem was believed to be the center of the earth is alluded to in vs. 5, but not to glorify her. Rather, Ezekiel pictures a kind of theatre-in-the round, with the nations as the spectators of Jerusalem's thoroughgoing humiliation. What is so special about this city, he claims, is that she has been worse than any other (vss. 6–7), and correspondingly, her punishment will also be worse than any other's (vs. 9). The first message of Ezekiel's to be recorded in the book is thus a ferocious attack on Zion-theology, the conviction that Jerusalem was God's chosen city where his presence could be encountered, a city especially blessed, preserved and protected by him. But now, God shows himself to be the enemy of Jerusalem, and that same message will be repeated by Ezekiel over and over, in a great variety of ways, as he tries to prepare the exiles to face the terrible reality which is imminent; the destruction of that beloved city.

Escape into Captivity (12:1–20)

In addition to that cluster of symbolic acts recorded near the beginning of the book, there are several others to be found in later chapters. This passage contains two which will be discussed together. Its introduction reminds us of Ezekiel's call, with its reference to the rebellious house. If the passage is to be dated perhaps a year or two later than the symbolic acts recorded earlier, as seems likely, then the reference is a significant one. It indicates that no change has yet occurred, despite all of Ezekiel's efforts. Yet there does appear a glimmer of hope, in vs. 3—"Perhaps they will understand, though they are a rebellious house"—and that is more than we have found so far in the book. We know that eventually the message of what God was really doing in all this did get through to them, but the indications are that this did not happen until after 587.

Ezekiel's activities would have brought back painful memories. He gathers up as many of his belongings as he can carry on his back, making sure that he has an audience, then digs a hole through the (mud brick) wall of his house, crawls through at night-fall, and leaves the community. Next morning he has obviously returned and is ready to explain why he had done this. It has been an ambiguous action this time and so the question of the spectators, "What are you doing?" is recorded, for it might very well have been a sign that each of them would soon gather up his belongings and begin the trip back to the Promised Land. But there is no good news in Ezekiel's interpretation: "I am a sign for you: as I have done, so shall it be done to them; they shall go into exile, into captivity" (vs. 11). It is another message about the near future of Jerusalem. The interpretation continues in what some think to be a later expansion, to refer quite specifically to the attempted escape of King Zedekiah ("the prince who is among them") and his subsequent capture (2 Kings 25:4–7). Once again a brief indication of what purpose God intends to accomplish by all this is added in vs. 16: "that they may confess all their abominations among the nations where they go, and may know that I am the Lord," but even that is still put in rather negative terms.

This act presumably did not cause any great hardship for the prophet, as some of the others did, but once again we see evidence that a prophet is expected to participate in the experiences of his people in Jerusalem even when he is separated from them physically. It may have also served as an object lesson, forcing the exiles to consider the possibility of another catastrophe in Jerusalem, the next one even worse than the one they went through.

The extreme physical effects of the prophetic commission on Ezekiel reappear in vss. 17–20, in which the trembling of the fugitives from Jerusalem is reproduced in the prophet's own behavior. Their terror and grief and fatigue is felt by Ezekiel, either as he deliberately acts out his eating and drinking "with trembling and with fearfulness," or perhaps by this time it has become a state over which he has little control, so thoroughly has his own life become identified with those deadly events which are approaching Jerusalem.

The Delight of Your Eyes (24:15–17)

According to the date at the beginning of this chapter, it is 587 B.C., and Jerusalem is once again under seige. Ezekiel's

words have begun to come true, and at some time near the
end of the war he is ordered to perform another symbolic act.
He is warned that on that day his wife, "the delight of your
eyes," will die, but for a prophet even that cannot be a pri-
vate event. As Ezekiel was about to lose the delight of his
eyes, so also Israel was losing the delight of its eyes, that
magnificent temple Solomon had built in Jerusalem, the
place Yahweh had chosen to make his name to dwell there
(vs. 21). But on the day when that temple was looted and
burnt there would be no chance for mourning in Jerusalem.
Those who had trusted in it would be running for their lives,
hiding in fear, suffering pain and despair and terror. And in
Babylonia the exiles would be going about their daily busi-
ness, unaware that they had lost the one thing on which they
had based their last hopes. Once again, to be a prophet
makes one different from every other person; for if Ezekiel's
people could not mourn the loss of the delight of their eyes,
then neither could he. No longer does he perform symbolic
acts in order to try to get a point across, for soon there will be
no more argument about the inviolability of Jerusalem. But
he must be a sign to them (vs. 24), that is, his obedient behavior as a man of God to the word of God which comes through
his lips stands over against them daily as the sign that the
word which he speaks is true.

We have heard Ezekiel complain only once, when he was
asked to violate his priestly commitment (4:14). No great emphasis is put on his obedience elsewhere, he just does what
God orders him to do, and accepts the personal consequences. This has made him seem cold and forbidding to
some interpreters but there are indications here and there
that this was a man whose feelings were strong, but kept
very firmly under control. What he felt that day is hinted at
in two ways, by the very expression "delight of your eyes,"
and by the warning,"Sigh, but not aloud." His obedience is
nowhere expressed more impressively than by the simple
statement in vs. 18, after he hears the worst message God
could ever speak to him: Today your wife will die and Jerusalem will fall. "So I spoke to the people in the morning, and at
evening my wife died. And on the next morning I did as I was
commanded."

(There are minor symbolic acts recorded in 21:19–20 and

37:16–22, but since they do not contribute to the discussion of that aspect of Ezekiel's work, they will be treated within the context of those chapters.)

An Interpretation of Ezekiel's Symbolic Acts

At the beginning of this section the comment was made that in addition to the message to the exiles conveyed by the symbolic act, there was another message which the descendants of the exiles found in the life of the prophet himself. That has been hinted at in the discussion of individual passages and now an attempt will be made to spell it out more clearly. An Israelite prophet was sometimes called "man of God" (see 1 Kings 20:28), and that term is a helpful one to use here, for the prophetic experience pours a great deal of meaning into it.

The commission of the prophet explicitly made him a messenger, sent to deliver the word of God. But the stories of events in the lives of the prophets reveal that they were also something more than that. Sometimes they called themselves "signs," as in Isa 8:18, Ezek 12:11, and 24:24. There had to be found in their lives evidence of the truth of the messages they proclaimed, and sometimes it was their mere presence as an obedient individual which was the sign, but there was more to it than that.

As a man of God, the prophet not only spoke for God, but was at times ordered to act the divine role symbolically. So Hosea found that because God's covenant partner had been perennially unfaithful, it would also be necessary for him, as the man of God, to have an unfaithful marriage partner (Hos 1:2), and so also Ezekiel set his face against that model of Jerusalem under seige and methodically destroyed the hair which symbolically represented its people: But the man of God does not only speak for God and symbolically assume the relationship to the people which is properly God's for he is also a member of that people. Being called to prophesy did not set him apart from them so that he was wholly on God's side, rather it seemed to reaffirm his oneness with Israel. One of the traditional prophetic functions was intercession (see Amos 7:1–6): standing on the side of the people to appeal on their behalf to God. And when God forbade them to intercede, as was the case with Jeremiah, then prophets began to

experience more and more intensely the very judgment
which they had proclaimed against Israel. Note that there
are no sectarians among the prophets, none who withdraw
and call to themselves a pure and faithful group who are expected to avoid the coming judgment. Israel is going to be
judged, and the man of God must be there, to share in it. So
Jeremiah is forbidden ever to marry and have children, because the children borne in Jerusalem in his time are going
to die (Jer 16:1–4), and he is not permitted to participate in
funerals or in celebrations, for all normalcy will soon be impossible for everyone (16:5–13). And Ezekiel must try to subsist on near starvation rations—amid the peace of the exilic
community in Babylonia—because people in Jerusalem are
starving, he must reenact their futile attempts to escape, and
he may not mourn his beloved wife because all the normal
mourning customs are impossible for those in Jerusalem that
day.

Why does God treat them so, those whom he has called to
his special service, who are obedient in the midst of rebellion? Why should not they be given all special privileges in
order to show that it is right to obey? The account of Ezekiel
lying on his side goes further than any other in explaining
why, when God says, "I will lay the punishment of the house
of Israel upon you, for the number of days that you lie upon
it, you shall bear their punishment" (4:4). What other
passages have only hinted at this one makes explicit; that the
prophet is called to endure a kind of vicarious suffering. Note
that vicarious can be used in more than one way. This is not
suffering *instead of*, as we use the term to refer to the death of
Christ, but suffering *along with*, even though the vicarious
sufferer has done nothing to deserve it. It is participation in
the full experience of one's people without claiming any special rights because of one's calling or superior obedience.
That is the special status of the man of God.

Why treat those obedient prophets so harshly? The anonymous and mysterious Servant of the Lord in Isaiah 53 takes
the idea which is just beginning to surface in the symbolic
acts of Jeremiah and Ezekiel, and which is only stated explicitly in Ezek 4:4–8, and carries it a step further to say, "Upon
him was the chastisement that made us whole, and with his
stripes we are healed" (Isa 53:5). But of what human being

could that be said? In the OT world, what is said of Ezekiel in chapter 4 and of the Suffering Servant in Isaiah 53 doesn't quite make sense. What else can be happening here, but an intimation of the necessity of incarnation? In the prophet, the side of God and the side of human beings were trying somehow to come together. God's way of approaching his people was not to stand over against, just to pronounce judgment and offer rewards, but to push toward divine participation in their whole lives, including the sharing of the just punishment which he had to inflict. In the sufferings of those special men of God are hints that God also intends to experience the suffering himself, but of course since they were only human beings that could not really happen, and the best they could be was a sign. In some of the symbolic acts the OT seems to be pushing toward an identification of God with human beings in the figure of the man of God, but it reaches a limit beyond which human beings cannot go. Is it not struggling to say something which can finally be said only by incarnation?

SECTION 4.

Destruction Is Imminent and Inevitable
(Ezekiel 6:1—7:27; 12:21–28; 14:12–23; 21:1—22:31)

These passages will be discussed together because of two things they have in common: They all focus on the main message of chapters 1—24, which is the inevitability of the second fall of Jerusalem and they express the message in fairly straightforward terms, using traditional prophetic forms in Ezekiel's own special way. It is this second feature which sets them off from the many other passages which contain essentially the same message, for here we do not find much evidence of the most distinctive literary features of the book, i.e., visions, symbolic acts, and allegory. These are not unimportant texts, and some of them have considerable literary power, but they tend to be overshadowed by others which are more distinctive. Because they speak of the realities of war in blunt and brutal terms they provide an occasion to take up a crucial theological issue raised by the prophetic interpretation of history, and that is the relationship between human violence and the God of peace.

It is probable that few sermons are preached from the chapters in this group. What needs to be said to modern Christians from texts threatening the thorough destruction of ancient Judah? The answer is that isolated texts of this type are probably not preachable, but that they remain important as essential parts of the history of salvation so that their context gives them continuing value. In the book of Ezekiel, there is context enough supplied by the surrounding chapters, for this prophet carries us through the destruction to the time of rebuilding, so that the meaning of all that suffering begins to become apparent. The concluding paragraphs of this section will make some further comments on that. These messages were of vital importance for a certain period in Ezekiel's ministry, for they were his response to a futile and dead-end effort by the exiles to keep up their morale by assuring themselves that the Promised Land and Jerusalem were the surety that God was still with them. The prophet realized he had to demolish every hope built on those things which were rapidly passing away, to try to find some way to get them to accept the coming destruction as inevitable and just, so that they could begin life again in exile without recriminations.

Ezekiel's words remained important for Jews in the exile and in the post-exilic period because they had been accepted as the truth that what happened in the fall of Jerusalem was just and in accordance with the will of God. So these messages were completely valid for their time, and continued to be instructive for a long time to Jews who found that 587 had a very long aftermath. But what do they mean to us now? Two issues of importance will be introduced here which will be developed as the discussion of the section continues. The first is the question why it should be necessary for God to inflict all that suffering as a means to salvation? And the second is to ask about the implications of the biblical affirmation that God is actively involved in the affairs of nations, and whether we really believe that to be true today?

Again and again, in the first 24 chapters of the book, Ezekiel hammers away at one point: The destruction of Jerusalem and the Promised Land is imminent and inevitable. Why so much of this? The answers are to be found in the audience. Jeremiah's letter to the exiles (Jer 29) tells us something about the reason. From the letter we learn that there were other prophets in Babylonia in addition to Ezekiel (see Jer 29:8-9, 15-23) and since Jeremiah's message emphasizes that the exile will last 70 years (which is really saying to them, "You're not coming back!"), and advises that they should not consider themselves displaced persons but should settle down and make new lives for themselves in Babylonia, it is clear that those other prophets were trying to keep up morale by assuring them that any day now, they were going home. But Ezekiel knew that very soon there would be no place to go back to, and he had to try to prepare them for that.

He also had received word from Jerusalem of another faulty interpretation of what had happened in 597, on which he comments in 11:14-16. Those left in Jerusalem had concluded that maybe the prophets were right after all, and Nebuchadnezzar's victory was warranted by God as punishment for the sinners in their midst. And it's clear now who the sinners were—those who have gone into exile! We who are left must be the righteous remnant, they concluded, and we are safe here in Jerusalem forever. Both Jeremiah (chap. 24) and Ezekiel challenged that interpretation, for they knew that if there was to be any future at all, it would come out of the exile experience. All the more reason for Ezekiel to try to establish a foundation which the coming deluge would not completely wash away. These dreadful chapters are thus a part of his pastoral work, as strange as that may seem, for they are a response to his people's most serious need.

Two important strands of OT theology are the bases for the problem with which Ezekiel struggled. The first was the promise of the land, which was traced all the way back to Abraham (see Gen 12:7; compare Exod 3:6–8). Despite the curses in Leviticus 26 and Deuteronomy 28, which contain threats of exile (probably only dating from the seventh or sixth centuries), it is likely that most Israelites believed the promise of the land to be an unconditional one, and thought of exile as virtual abrogation of the covenant. Faced by exile, then, they would have seen two options: a quick return to the Promised Land, or the end of their religion. Ezekiel tries to offer another: a better theology.

The second strand was Zion theology, which taught that Yahweh had chosen David and his family to rule over Israel and Zion as the place where he would make his name to dwell (see Pss 132; 48). Because of the miraculous deliverance of Jerusalem from the armies of Sennacherib in 701 B.C., Zion theology had been infused, during the seventh century, with the belief in the virtual invulnerability of Jerusalem (see Jeremiah's challenge to that in Jer 7). Now, that belief must have been sorely shaken when Nebuchadnezzar successfully besieged and captured the city in 597, but beliefs die hard and it appears that exiles expected that Yahweh would soon intervene to avenge that terrible insult, destroy Nebuchadnezzar, and restore them to their homes. The intensity of those hopes colored everything they heard from Ezekiel's lips, and it is with the potency of that wishful thinking, expressed in two of the exiles' proverbs, that we need to begin our consideration of the individual passages.

He Prophesies of Times Far Off (12:21–28)

In those times it is astonishing that complacency could have been a problem, and yet it was. Here is the last defense put up by wishful thinking, two sayings repeated so often they have become virtual proverbs in that community of exiles. The first, "The days grow long, and every vision comes to naught," might well have been the result of hearing first one prophet, then another, whose messages did not coincide and sometimes were contradictory, until the people finally began to weary and to wonder whether one could count on any of it. Ezekiel's answer is that false prophecy will soon come to an end and the truth of his words will soon be demonstrated by what God himself is about to do.

The second proverb is not quite so skeptical in tone, but has the same effect, which is to devalue anything Ezekiel says. "The vision that he sees is for many days hence, and he prophesies of times far off." Certainly they had a prophet in their midst and what a prophet said might just come true, some day. But not now, nothing to worry about now! In response to Ezekiel's efforts to get them to think about the unacceptable this was the final refuge for their complacency. There is evidence that he faced outright hostility at times, as well, but these proverbs show that one of his perennial struggles was with those who just wouldn't take him seriously. That helps us to understand not only why he said the same thing so many times over, but also to appreciate the measures he was willing to take to find new forms for the message; to seduce them, if you will, to listen to something they had no intention of accepting. As far as we can tell, from studying the whole book, Ezekiel had no more success than his precedessors in creating a group of understanding, committed, and faithful people whose faith was based on anything more secure and lasting than the endurance of Jerusalem and its temple. That seems to be the case, because after 587 we find him having to cope with cynicism, bitterness, and despair.

Ezekiel's congregation was not unusual. It was a typical reaction. When we are threatened by change, when what we have always depended on begins to appear shaky, when we should then be realistic and acknowledge that things are not going to be the same again and that we ought to be planning how to meet the new situation, then our typical response is often not so different from that of the exiles: vigorously pulling up the covers and saying, It isn't so; it's all a mistake; everything is going to be all right. It should not be hard for us, then, to understand the exiles' attitude, or to appreciate Ezekiel's dilemma.

What Have They Done to My Land? (6:1–14)

In the history of Ezekiel research, there came a time when many scholars believed that since the prophet not only spoke regularly about Jerusalem and Judah, but also spoke *to* them, therefore, Jerusalem is where he must have been, not in exile. What sense would these words make in Babylonia, they asked, and for a time the theory of a Palestinian ministry with a later editing of his words to make them applicable to exile, and the theory of a ministry beginning in Palestine and concluding in Babylonia vied for favor. But continuing research has found a better answer. He spoke almost daily about Jerusalem because that is all the exiles had on their minds and he sometimes addressed his words to the mountains and the city because that is where their hearts were. Before they could begin to cope with exile something had to be done about that fixation on their homeland. So in this chapter he speaks to the mountains of Israel from the plains of Mesopotamia. It is a direct reference to the fact that for Israel the land was more than just a place to live, it was a part of their theology. But now, Ezekiel says it will not even be a place to live, but a place to die. He speaks to the mountains not only because they dominated the topography of Judah and would be among the fondest memories of those now living in a flat land, but because on the mountains were the "high places," the old Canaanite sanctuaries which Israel had taken over and partly converted to the worship of Yahweh, but where the spirit of the gods of Canaan was still very much alive. King Josiah's reform, early in the seventh century (see 2 Kings 22—23) had come and gone and things were no better than they had ever been. So Ezekiel sees corpses in the high places and corpses in the cities, a land of death (vss. 3–7, 11–14). It should not have been unimaginable to his audience, for they had been through a war, but what makes this message so hard is that it claims the same thing they had experienced is going to happen again, and it is going to be appallingly complete!

Yet in the midst of the chapter we hear of a remnant (vss. 8–10). It is an important paragraph, even though it has nothing to do with our ideas of the faithful remnant, for it does provide, early in the book, a little clue that there may be something to all this destruction beyond judgment and punishment. It is an unfaithful remnant which he expects to escape the general slaughter, but as they are scattered among the nations Ezekiel believes something will happen to them which will finally begin to change them. They will "remember" God, and then they will "be loathesome in their own sight," when they finally acknowledge that they are the problem, and not God, and "they shall know that I am the Lord." The remembering here is obviously an active thing, far more than some wistful recollection of the good, old days. It is the internal acceptance of the truth about who God really is and of what their relationship to him must be. So repentance is the natural result of "remembering," because what they have done is to substitute the land itself and concerns for its productivity (nature religion) in the place of the one God who has given it all to them. But why are such drastic measures needed to get that message across? We shall continue to struggle with that question in the suceeding chapters.

The End of Israel (7:1–27)

In some of the most vivid language in the book, Ezekiel takes up a theme of Amos which is in a sense the central theme of all judgment prophecy, although few dared to state it so bluntly: "The end has come upon my people Israel" (Amos 8:2). It is a terrifying passage, if taken seriously, for it moves now beyond the fall of one city to speak of a cataclysm which affects the four corners of the earth (not just the land of Palestine, see Ezek 7:2). The tendency toward a universalizing of the coming judgment in this chapter can be explained by the appearance of the Day of the Lord theme (note vss. 7, 10, 12) which had already been given a broad scope by earlier prophets. (Compare especially the first chapter of

Zephaniah.) Ezekiel's priestly background may also be revealed in his use of the term "end," for the Priestly Source of the Pentateuch speaks of another universal judgment, the Flood, in much the same way. "And God said to Noah, 'I have determined to make an end of all flesh; for the earth is filled with violence through them; behold, I will destroy them with the earth' " (Gen 6:13). There are conflicting theories about the origins of the Day of the Lord concept which need not concern us at this point, but the one which claims it was originally the Day of Yahweh's victory over his enemies on the battlefield fits this chapter better than any other because of its vivid description of the horrors of war in vss. 14–27. Its original intent, in speaking so brutally, was to get people to consider the inconceivable— "I will turn my face from them, that they may profane my precious place" (7:22). But for us there seems to be little to preach from the chapter except in connection with the whole story of exile and restoration or in consideration of the problem of war in the plan of God (to be discussed further at the conclusion of this section). It is one of the most extreme interpretations of the fall of Jerusalem to be found anywhere in the Bible. Although Amos had dared to speak of "an end" of his people Israel back in the eighth century, and the prophets who followed him did speak in radical terms of the changes which they believed God was about to bring in, the word "end" may have sounded a bit too final. But Ezekiel needs the shock effect, for one thing, and he is living through it—seeing everything actually come to an end. Furthermore, his interpretation of it will involve a theology of death and resurrection, taking the word "end" with the utmost seriousness. Another possible use of this chapter 7 might then be as background to chapter 37, which speaks of exile as death.

None Righteous, No Not One (14:12–23)

Isn't there some way to avert, or at least to mitigate the terrible judgment which Ezekiel says is coming soon? After all, Abraham interceded for Sodom, and Moses more than once found ways to persuade God not to destroy his people when they rebelled in the wilderness. One of the traditional roles of the prophet was to serve as intercessor, as well. But God had already warned Jeremiah that he was not to attempt to intercede for his people, for it was too late for that (Jer 7:16), and added that even the great heroes of the past, Moses and Samuel, would be able to do nothing, this time (Jer 15:1). Ezekiel takes up the same theme in this passage in a kind of litany of destruction. If famine comes (vss. 13–14), if wild beasts multiply (vss. 15–16), if a sword goes through the land (vss. 17–18), or if a pestilence comes (vss. 19–20)—all of them the result of their sinfulness, as the introduction shows (vs. 13), not even the most famous paragons of righteousness of the past, Noah, Daniel, and Job, would be able to do anything to save any life but their own. The choice of that particular trio used to be a problem, because the only Daniel known to us was a younger contemporary of Ezekiel, and he didn't seem to fit. Now, however, the Ugaritic texts from Ras Shamra (Syria) have provided evidence that there was a legendary king, Dan'el, who was famous for his righteousness but who was unable to save the life of his son. If this is the figure to whom Ezekiel is referring, then he has chosen three legendary characters from the distant past, all of them non-Israelites, all of whom were remembered to have lost children. The concept of corporate responsibility, which will be discussed at length in connection with chapter 18, and which acknowledged that sometimes one person's righteousness could bring blessings for others who had done nothing to deserve them, is denied at this point by Ezekiel. There is no hope. The fact is, Noah, Daniel, and Job aren't around, or anyone like them, as vss. 21–23 show. Once again we hear of an unfaithful remnant, in vs. 22, and Ezekiel says to those already in exile, if you have any inclination to complain about the injustice of what is coming, when you see what the survivors are like, you will realize that the completeness of the judgment just corresponds to the thoroughness of the corruption in the land you left behind. There is none righteous, no not one, or as Ezekiel puts it in 22:30: "And I sought for a man among them who should build up the wall and stand in the breach before me for the land, that I should not destroy it; but I found none." This is another variation on the perennial theme of the first part of the book.

God Himself Wields the Sword (21:1–32)

This chapter contains three separate oracles, each taking the sword as its main theme, and so in the editing of the book they have appropriately been associated with one another. In the first, Ezekiel is once again to address the land of Israel with a most shocking word. God himself is about to wield the sword against them—using the old Israelite concept of Yahweh the warrior (Exod 15:3)—and it will "cut off from you both righteous and wicked" (vs. 3). How could such a thing be said about the work of God? It is true, of course, that this is exactly what happens in war, and so we shall add this statement to the evidence which will be discussed in the conclusion to this section. It must be noted carefully, however, that God is by no means depicted as doing this willingly or taking any pleasure in vengeance, for his representative on earth is to deliver these words sighing "with breaking heart and bitter grief" (vs. 6). The tension which judgment of his people creates within God himself is reflected in the actions which Ezekiel is ordered to perform in this chapter. In vs. 14 he is to clap his hands as a sign of anger (see vs. 17), but vs. 6 shows that along with anger goes bitter grief.

The second passage (vss. 8–17) is strongly poetic in flavor, a bitter song of the sword, but again reflecting mixed emotions. The bitterness appears in the accusation that the rod, the usual means of discipline, has been completely ineffective (vs. 10b), so now comes the sword, and that is not disciplinary but quite another matter (vs. 13). But as Ezekiel pronounces the words he is also ordered by God to cry and wail and smite his thigh, for this is a loss to God and his prophet as well as to the rebellious people.

The third passage (vss. 18–32) might have been included with the symbolic acts, for it begins that way, but the action itself is relatively insignificant compared to the others. The sword is now historified and put into the hand of Nebuchadnezzar, who has evidently, at the time this was uttered, just set out on that final campaign against Jerusalem. The question is which of the rebels he will attack first, Judah or the Ammonites, and Ezekiel's answer is that he is heading directly for Jerusalem. Once again, the effect of the message is, there is no hope. And in case anyone might deduce from the original oracle that somehow the Ammonites would be successful in their rebellion, at some time a message concerning the sword which would also be wielded against them was added to the Babylon passage (vss. 28–32). For comments on the place of the nations in Ezekiel's theology see section 10.

Rotten to the Core (22:1–31)

This is an extended indictment of Jerusalem, using two images, blood as a symbol of both ethical and ritual crimes, and the dross which is the useless part of the smelting process. The general accusations which Ezekiel has been making against Jerusalem and Judah now become very specific, with the citation of a gamut of violations of Israel's traditional law. Each of the two parts of the chapter follows the same pattern; he begins with an image, blood in vss. 2–4 and smelting in vss. 18–22, continues with an extensive indictment in vss. 6–12 and vss. 23–30, concluding each part with the pronouncement of the sentence in vss. 13–16 and 31. The sentence in vs. 15 brings the whole story home to Ezekiel's audience, for it is what Israel thought of as the ultimate tragedy, and it had become reality for them: "I will scatter you among the nations and disperse you through the countries." But something is added, and that is what they had not quite comprehended as yet: "and I will consume your filthiness out of you." In these terrible passages, it is only the presence of a few, brief statements such as this that enabled the exiles eventually to make theological sense of them, and it is to our efforts to incorporate them into our theology that we must now turn.

Can It Be Our God Who Says and Does Such Things?

Perhaps it is not quite as bad as it sounds, when Ezekiel announces that God will "cut off from you both righteous and wicked" (21:3), for commentators suggest this is an example of comprehending the whole of something by referring to its two extremes (such as "from top to bottom" or "man and beast"), but that does not really solve the problem created for us when it is said that God wills all this terror and destruction. Obviously the issue cannot be dealt with at length here, but it must be taken up if we are to be able to make any sort of responsible use of these texts. Let us approach the subject by asking three "skeptical questions."

(1). Was Israel *that* bad? Could it really have been necessary for God to give up on the whole system—covenant, law,

priesthood, kingship, and all the rest—so as to start over
from zero?

The prophets' answer to the question is that Israel was
much worse than any of its neighbors. In Ezekiel's allegory of
Jerusalem as the unfaithful wife we find, "As I live, says the
Lord God, your sister Sodom and her daughters have not
done as you and your daughters have done" (16:48). Jerusalem was worse than Sodom. Elsewhere he begins a judgment
speech: "Because you are more turbulent than the nations
that are round about you" (5:7). But that is not the conclusion we would reach from making a dispassionate comparison of the way Israel and her neighbors lived. Compared to
the Egyptians and the Hittites and the Phoenicians and the
Assyrians and the Babylonians they were, by our standards,
no worse and in many ways much better. But the prophets
did not make such a dispassionate comparison. They did not
analyze the way a sociologist would analyze. They did not
really, in fact, compare Israel's lifestyle with that of their
neighbors, but compared Israel's lifestyle with the standards
which Yahweh had given Israel. Those standards were much
higher than those accepted by any of their neighbors, and
Israel's behavior fell correspondingly lower. That was the basis for the judgment. "You only have I known of all the families of the earth, therefore I will punish you for all your
iniquities," Amos said (3:2); and the point of that was the
same as Jesus' point when he said, "Every one to whom
much is given, of him will much be required" (Luke 12:48).
Israel had every chance to do something sensational, and
they muffed it. Their responsibilities before God were thus
heavier than those of any other people, as the prophets saw
it, and so they were judged according to what they were
given. Our answer, then, to the question, Was Israel that
bad? is, by impartial standards, No; but we do expect more
of those who have been given more, considering that to be
only fair, so how can we quibble with God for expecting the
same?

(2). Wouldn't Jerusalem have fallen anyway, no matter
how good Israel was? Why should we think the successes of
Assyria and Babylonia were the result of Israel's low moral
standards, and not simply due to the fact that the former had
bigger and better armies?

The only valid answer to that one is: We don't know whether Jerusalem would have fallen anyway, even if they had all repented and had become the perfect society, because to imagine that is to begin to write historical fiction. All we really know is, that didn't happen. But our inclinations toward naturalistic readings of history incline us to say that surely the empire building activities of Assyria and Babylonia would have led them to and through Palestine, no matter what Israel did. Why should we see their activities as a work of divine judgment, and not just the result of being located in a very unfortunate geographical position?

What can we say in response to this almost instinctive modern reaction to the prophetic interpretation of history?

First, we must remind ourselves that nothing can be pronounced impossible in history. Some most improbable, and on the human level unexplainable, things have really happened. So we cannot say, it is impossible that Israel could have been saved if they had changed their ways. All we can honestly say is that we don't know.

But once again let me remind you that this comes close to writing historical fiction, discussing what in fact did not happen. Let us simply concentrate on what *did* happen:

> Israel and Judah did fail to live up to the standards held up for them in the covenant.
>
> Israel and Judah did fall to the Assyrians and Babylonians.
>
> The exiled Judeans did accept the prophetic judgment as true. Eventually they were willing to admit that Ezekiel and his predecessors were right; that what happened to them was a result of their rebellion against their God.
>
> As a result, they did repent and they did begin to change their ways. The result of exile was a new people.
>
> And so history was changed because of the belief of those people that the exile was the deserved punishment for their sins.

Try historical fiction again; what if they had concluded: We are exiles because the Babylonians had a better army? If they had, then it really would have been the end. Even though we may have trouble believing that God justly brought all this upon them it is gospel to us that *they* believed it.

(3). Can all this killing, raping, burning, and destruction really be the way God chose to accomplish his purpose? Can we accept the suffering of guilty and innocent alike as the will of God, necessary in order that this new, faithful people could be created? Could anything be worth that? If God has all the power Ezekiel claimed he had, couldn't he have found a better way?

Consider this answer: We cannot believe God *chooses* cruelty. The God we know stands in judgment of all that—killing, raping, burning, and destruction—so he surely does not will it. But in this world all those things happen. No one has yet been able to give an adequate explanation of why they happen, but they do. What Ezekiel is saying, and the rest of the Bible confirms, is that God in his wisdom finds ways to use even those evil deeds, of which he stands in judgment, in order to accomplish some good things.

Even war produces some good results, but the good things which come out of the activities of most conquering armies tend to be relatively small: acts of personal heroism or of kindness, in the midst of great suffering. But on this one occasion, God took the familiar activities of world-conquering armies, most of which cause us to cringe, and brought world-changing results of them.

Maybe Assyria and Babylonia would have come anyway. Many other conquerors have marched through Palestine and they are only two out of a long list. But no other conquest produced these results. Every other nation in the history of the Middle East has experienced the same disasters as Judah experienced. But no other nation but Judah came out of it reborn.

Because prophets had been saying that God was doing a new thing with Judah, because some Judeans believed that and that belief changed their lives, somehow (and how can we avoid saying God himself was acting in the "somehow") a new people was born out of all that agony. We cannot explain why it had to be that way; it is hard to believe it is God's favorite way, but we do know that in spite of all that suffering, or—who knows?—maybe because of all that suffering, something good came into the world. We are close to the theology of the cross in all this.

The reason which God had for bringing that old era to an end was not, then, for punishment or for revenge or because he had finally given up on humanity; but to start over, with a new people under a new covenant in a new world. The nations did as nations do, but God found a way to transmute their evil into his good.

A Vision of Old Jerusalem
(Ezekiel 8:1—11:25)

This is a section filled with difficulties, and for a full discussion of the problems and proposed solutions you will need to consult the commentaries, since they are not issues which are likely to have a significant effect on the homiletical use of these chapters. The section makes a valuable contribution to the development of the thought of the book, but is not likely to be used much for preaching since its message is very much focused on a particular situation in Israel's history. For the most part the interpretation offered here will have in mind the usefulness of these chapters in reinforcing messages which are presented in more preachable form elsewhere.

Some of the major problems must at least be listed, as we begin, for no intelligent reading of the passage is possible without taking them seriously. The section has a clear beginning and end; Ezekiel is in his house with elders sitting before him, in 8:1, when he falls into a trance and is transported to Jerusalem, and in 11:24–25 he is returned to the exiles and reports his vision to them. But the unity of what intervenes is questionable in places. The detailed description of the throne chariot in chapter 10 interrupts the progress of the vision and it is hard to understand what contribution it is supposed to make at this point. The vision of the twenty-five princes of the people in 11:1–21 shows no awareness of what has just preceded, namely the annihilation of the most of the population of Jerusalem, which raises questions about whether it was originally a part of the larger vision or was at one time a separate unit. If it does properly belong with chapters 8—9, then it seems likely that something which would show their original relationship has been lost. Other difficulties include a text which is poorly transmitted in places, words and expressions (such as the infamous "branch to the nose") which no one is quite sure how to translate much less understand, the vagueness of the description of the pagan customs in chapter 8, which makes their identification uncertain, and the problem of understanding exactly what happened to Ezekiel when he was taken by a lock of his head and lifted up between earth and heaven. Since that is the most striking of all his ecstatic experiences, this seems the appropriate place to add something to what was said about this subject in section 1.

Ezekiel's Paranormal Experiences

In addition to the gift of seeing and hearing things which other people do not perceive, Ezekiel found that his ecstatic experiences had physical effects upon him which are mentioned only a few times in stories of other prophets and which are unique in some cases. He apparently fainted dead away when he saw the throne chariot (1:28), sat in a stupor in his house for seven days thereafter (3:15), was unable to speak at times (3:26; 24:27; 33:22), felt that God had put cords upon him so that he could not move (3:25; 4:8), spoke of the "hand of the Lord" being upon him (3:22), and in this section tells us that the figure of a man "put forth the form of a hand, and took me by a lock of my head; and the Spirit lifted me up between earth and heaven, and brought me in visions of God to Jerusalem." The first issue in all this is to be sure, if we can, what he actually claims. Is this instantaneous transportation, bodily, from place to place? Certainly there is no support in Hebrew thought for thinking he speaks of some disembodied existence in which he could travel from Babylonia to Jerusalem. Or, does the phrase "visions of God" provide the clue that he stayed where he was but in his trance was able to see in considerable detail what was happening far away in Jerusalem? No one can be sure of the answer to the question, of course, but the last suggestion seems to fit what Ezekiel tells us about the experience better than the others. Whether one believes that such things really happen is a matter for individual decision. All of Ezekiel's experiences have parallels in claims made by ecstatic personalities in most of the religions of the world, and even by non-religious people in our own day. No doubt some of them were lying, but research into parapsychology in recent times is beginning to suggest that not every such claim can be dismissed as impossible, and Ezekiel's experiences are certainly not to be explained as the result of severe mental illness, as several writers have attempted to prove. It is strongly to be urged that in preaching from passages such as this the paranormal aspect be allowed for (not explained away) but not be emphasized as if these marvels were the point of the passage or the proof of its authenticity. The message is always something other than the fact that such an experience happened to a certain person, for the experience only functions to point to a more significant reality in which all can share.

Old Jerusalem—The Diagnosis

Ezekiel has been speaking in general terms about the corruption to be found within Jerusalem and the rebellious nature of the people. As we continue through the book we shall find both subjects developed in more detail, and in this section the former is presented in a highly picturesque manner, as an eyewitness account of things which presumably the exiles would already know something about. Whether the syncretistic form of Yahwism as it was practiced in the Jerusalem temple had grown worse in the six years since they had left the city we do not know, but what Ezekiel describes certainly cannot all have been a novelty to the exiles. How many of them would have defended these practices as what had always been done in the practice of their religion and how many considered them to be irregular and to be avoided, we also cannot judge, but one of the intended effects of this passage is surely to make it clear to them that all of this stands under the judgment of Yahweh and that its continuance makes it certain that Jerusalem will soon be destroyed.

Syncretism was nothing new, for there is evidence that from the beginning of life in Canaan the Israelites borrowed beliefs and practices from the Canaanites without considering whether they were compatible with the essence of Yahwism. For example, a good Yahwist such as David gave one of his sons the name Beeliada, which means "Baal knows" (1 Chron 14:6), and when Elijah insisted that his people could not worship both Yahweh and Baal, the insistence that they had to make a choice seems to have been a new idea to them (1 Kings 18:21). We are told that early in the monarchy Solomon's wives introduced foreign cults into Jerusalem, and in the Assyrian period the vassal kings who ruled Judah under foreign overlords found it either necessary or politic to add the worship of Assyrian deities to the variety already present in the capital city. Josiah's reform, late in the seventh century, seems to have been short-lived, and his untimely death probably convinced a good many that he had been a fanatic and wrong.

The identity of some of the cults which Ezekiel saw in his vision of the temple is uncertain. Tammuz is known to be a Mesopotamian deity whose death and sojourn in the netherworld are the basis for the rites of weeping mentioned in 8:14, and the worship of the sun was to be found in virtually every culture (8:14). But the "image of jealousy" is not described, so it might be the Canaanite goddess Asherah (2 Kings 21:7), but we cannot be sure of that. Since the Egyptians made more use of animal figures to represent their deities than any of the other surrounding peoples, the cult described in 8:7–12 may have been borrowed from there, but again there is nothing specific enough to make the identification certain. The most important element in this chapter is another of the quotations which play such an important role in the book, this one explaining the attitude of those who come to Yahweh's temple to worship other deities: "The Lord does not see us, the Lord has forsaken the land" (8:12). It is outright apostasy, not just syncretism, which Ezekiel witnesses. Those exiles who grounded their whole future in their belief in Yahweh's presence in the temple must have been profoundly shaken by this description of the occupation of his house by foreign gods and the presence in it of people who really did not believe in him at all any more. The effect of the report of this vision on the exiles should have been to force them to face facts which explained why Jerusalem was soon to fall again, and its value for us is that those same facts help us to understand why so drastic a change in the relationship between God and Israel as exile had become essential.

Although the cultic irregularities which were being practiced in the temple itself must have been extremely distressing to the priest, Ezekiel, that was not the full extent of the problem. Without warning, at the end of chapter 8, we hear about filling the land with violence (see also 9:9), and we can then see the value of having 11:1–12 associated with this vision, even though it may originally have belonged in another context, for that passage spells out in some detail the existence of what seems to have been a reign of terror carried out by the "princes of the people," who obviously wielded a great deal of control over the city during the period from 597 to 587. The familiar prophetic condemnation of injustice is not foreign to Ezekiel, as we see in other chapters as well (for example, chap. 22) and the appearance of the two requirements of God here, true worship and doing justice, reminds us of the biblical insistence that the two cannot be separated.

Old Jerusalem—The Prognosis

The vision of Jerusalem is a combination of (1) people and events which presumably anyone standing there could have witnessed and (2) other beings who are not part of the visible world, who participate in events which had not happened yet. These are additional features which make chapters 8—11 the most unusual passage in the book. Elsewhere Ezekiel speaks of the destruction of Jerusalem in essentially realistic terms, by fire, sword, famine, and pestilence, but here he sees supernatural beings of some kind, carrying weapons which are not described, who are ordered to carry out a mass execution, sparing only those who are appalled at the apostasy practiced in their midst. Nothing like that happened during the sixth year of the exile, the time of Ezekiel's vision, so that part of it was predictive of the future. The prognosis for Jerusalem, then, is death for its inhabitants and burning for the city (10:2), and the worst thing about it is that the executioners are to begin at the spot considered so holy it was invulnerable—the temple itself (9:6–7). Despite Ezekiel's earlier warnings, the thought of that is so devastating that he cries out in dismay, "Ah, Lord God! wilt thou destroy all that remains of Israel in the outpouring of thy wrath upon Jerusalem?" (9:8). The same cry is repeated in 11:13, when he sees the death of Pelatiah, and in that chapter an answer is provided. It is a response to another quote from those left behind in Jerusalem after 597, "They have gone far from the Lord; to us this land is given for a possession" (11:15). That is, some of the people of Jerusalem had concluded the exile had sorted out the sinners from their midst, who were now getting what they deserved in Babylon, while they who were left behind must obviously be the righteous remnant, to whom belonged the Promised Land and the future. Jeremiah spoke against the same attitude (Jer 24), with a message much the same as what Ezekiel says in this chapter. Commentators differ on whether Ezek 11:14–21 are best understood as originally a part of the vision report, or whether it is more likely that a promise delivered after 587 was later added to the vision in order to show that in spite of the destruction of Jerusalem God still had a future in mind which he would bring about by working with the community in exile. Although the majority of scholars favor the latter opinion, there is something to be said for the interpretation of these verses as a response to a very desperate need on the part of exiles who did take Ezekiel's other words seriously in the years prior to 587. There were two things in what they were hearing about Jerusalem which were likely to lead them to utter despair. One was the report of the theologizing practiced by those left behind, as quoted in 11:15, which some of the exiles might be inclined to agree with. They felt cut off from Yahweh, his land and his people, and found it hard to believe there could be any future for them where they were. They wanted to think they could go back soon, but Ezekiel had been hammering away at the need to give up that hope. If they believed any of this, then their reaction must have been, What's the use? It really is all over for us! The question would be, then, how long Ezekiel could wait before giving some indication of a change for the better that they could hope for? Ten years would be a long time for a community to continue to exist with the kind of conflicting hopes, mingled with strands of bitterness and despair, which we find reflected in the book of Ezekiel. So it might be that the first indications of a promise which will not be spelled out in detail until after 587 were offered earlier in order to show the exiles where their attention ought to be concentrated. The distressing message that the glory of Yahweh had left Jerusalem (10:18–19; 11:23) can then be countered both by the assurance that Ezekiel had already seen it present in Mesopotamia (chaps. 1—3) and by God's reminder that he had already been a sanctuary to them for a while (or, in small measure, 11:16) in exile.

Conclusions

The major themes of this passage appear prominently elsewhere in the book. They are the certainty that Jerusalem will be destroyed, with the reasons why that is necessary, the freedom of Yahweh to leave his temple and to provide a sanctuary for his people anywhere he chooses, and the promise that there will be some left alive whom he had determined to change in order to make a future possible for them. The depth of the problem which has to be overcome is probably the major emphasis of the text, with its combination of quotations indicating outright apostasy (8:12) coupled with great self-assurance (11:15) in a place where both the cultic and ethical standards of Yahweh have been virtually forgotten.

Attractive Nuisances:
False Prophecy and
Idol Worship
(Ezekiel 13:1—14:11)

In this part of the book Ezekiel deals with three specific problems which have been created for the exilic community by people who hold positions of responsibility: prophets and elders. From Jeremiah's letter to the exiles (Jer 29) it is clear that there were several people in the community who were recognized as being prophets but from what Jeremiah had learned of their message, he condemned them as false prophets. They may have been the same people of whom Ezekiel speaks in 13:1–16, although, unlike Jeremiah, he does not name them and actually provides no personal information about them at all. He then takes up a quite different problem caused by some female prophets in their midst, who have added magic to their repertoire. Then we are introduced to one of the scenes in which Ezekiel's audience is specifically identified. "Certain of the elders of Israel" have come to inquire of the Lord from him, but Ezekiel is not permitted to perform that prophetic function. The Lord has instead a word of condemnation because of their continuing idolatrous practices. He had been warned in his call experience that he would face severe opposition to his work (2:3–7; 3:7–9); now we can see that in addition to the despondent exiles' natural inclination to disbelieve there were groups of people in positions of leadership who were advocating beliefs and practices which Ezekiel knew would ultimately be destructive of the community. He had no authority to deal with them except the word, but he had received a word from God which he sets over against them as the truth.

These fruitless options against which Ezekiel struggles have been labeled "attractive nuisances" here, but with no intention of suggesting they were unimportant, for what the law designates by that term can be responsible for a fatal accident. The commentaries point out how very carefully or-

ganized each of these three sections is; so it is clear that the
problems created by these groups were so important that the
prophet devoted special care to the way he dealt with them.
From our point of view they do appear to be very much
problems of the past, as we first read these passages, but on
reflection there is relevance in them for the present. We shall
see that some of the responsibilities of leadership at that
time do reappear as aspects of the responsibilities of contemporary leaders of the church. We are not prophets or elders
with functions identical to those in exile, and we do not
struggle much with the practice of magic or idolatry, but
there does appear in these texts a warning against temptations to take a popular route, as leaders, even though we
know that is a compromise with the truth.

False Prophecy (13:1–16)

There were prophets among the exiles who thought they
were fulfilling their calling by helping their people, but
Ezekiel says they have in fact been no help at all. They have
spoken falsehood, divined a lie, seen delusive visions, and
prophesied out of their own minds. The problem of how a
prophet could speak a word which presumably came from
God but was not the truth appears from time to time in the
OT from the ninth century on. Micaiah ben Imlah explained
the contradiction between his message and other prophets by
saying that Yahweh had sent a lying spirit to inspire them
with a message that was not true (1 Kings 22). Ezekiel may
be making a similar judgment about his rivals, acknowledg-
ing that they had seen visions, all right, but refusing to accept the existence of the phenomenon itself as proof of the
truth of the message. But he also follows Jeremiah's plan of
attack in questioning whether some of them had the ecstatic
experience at all. "Say to those who prophesy out of their
own minds," reminds us of Jeremiah's more explicit and
lengthy accusations that his contemporaries in Jerusalem
were claiming to have had dreams and visions when they
were only making it all up, and even, in their lack of ability,
were stealing oracles from one another (Jer 14:13–14;
23:16–18, 21–22, 25–32). The essence of what the false
prophets were doing wrong, according to both Jeremiah and
Ezekiel, was trying to comfort their people by proclaiming

an optimistic message when there were no realistic grounds for optimism—"saying, 'Peace,' when there is no peace" (Jer 6:14; 8:11; Ezek 13:10).

Besides bringing them an undeserved popularity, what was wrong with those efforts to cheer up people with promises of *shalom?* Ezekiel believes that what they are doing will make things worse for the people in the long run, for it is not offering them the kind of support they need to prepare them for the even more disheartening news which will soon come. So Ezekiel creates a series of vivid images to portray what is wrong with all this. Their popularity in a time of disaster makes them like the fox who builds a den in the ruins of a city and flourishes amid destruction. But what have they done which leads Ezekiel to say that they have not gone up into the breaches to defend their people? The answer comes in a third set of images, the whitewashed wall, a vivid picture filled with irony. The wall which the people have built is all their inadequate hopes and beliefs; it cannot stand against the storm which is about to break out. And what have these prophets done to help? They have given the rickety wall a coat of plaster or whitewash—a lot of strength that will add to it! But they aim to please, and they have given people what they want.

Magic (13:17–23)

Among the female prophets in exile were some who were more selective; they would offer what people wanted to those who would pay for it. There are some difficulties in understanding this passage, since Ezekiel refers to them as women who prophesy, but then does not speak of any specifically prophetic activity on their part. He deals with what some of them may have taken up as a sideline, magical practices about which we know very little. But note that he does not condemn them for being women prophets; that was an accepted thing in Israel (Exod 15:20; Jud 4:4; 2 Kings 22:14; Neh 6:14; Isa 8:3), and the judgment he makes here concerns only a perversion of prophecy. We do not know whether there were other "true prophets" in exile; the fact that Ezekiel does not mention them tells us nothing about that, for none of the prophets ever mentions a contemporary. Jeremiah and Ezekiel never refer to one another; neither do Amos and

Hosea or Isaiah and Micah. So for all we know there may have been others, male and female, who were as faithful as Ezekiel, but whose words either have been lost or have been preserved anonymously as additions to the books of other prophets.

The practice of magic had been condemned from early times in Israel, but was so popular in every other culture that it no doubt always maintained an underground presence, just as it continues to do to this day. But it is not just the truth or falsity of magical practices which concerns Ezekiel; he concentrates on the effect which the selling of charms is having on the morale of his people. "You have disheartened the righteous falsely, . . . and you have encouraged the wicked, that he should not turn from his wicked way to save his life" (13:22). The possibility of accepting Ezekiel's message, hard enough to believe even under the best of circumstances, was made even less likely by the offering of easy ways, techniques which could be bought, and the fact that there was a profit in it must have made those opponents all the more difficult to deal with.

Idolatry (14:1-11)

The elders who come to sit before Ezekiel are more evidence of the level of faithfulness of that remnant which went into exile. They obviously didn't intend to be apostates, giving up Yahweh completely, or they wouldn't have come to consult his prophet; but even so, they worship idols. Even the leaders of the community have not yet fully understood the true nature of the Yahwistic faith, and want to have a little of everything. What they came to inquire about is never revealed, instead Ezekiel simply quotes the law to them, as recent form-critical studies have shown. Verses 4-5 and 7-8 take the form of casuistic law, and vs. 9 can be compared with the law concerning the prophet who entices to idolatry in Deut 13:3 (and compare the whole of Deut 13 with this section). No new word from the prophet here, then, but only the citation of what the standards of the religion were supposed to be all along. The troublesome word, for us, "And if the prophet be deceived and speak a word, I, the Lord, have deceived that prophet" (vs. 9), probably means that any prophet who consents to participate in the activities of idolatrous people will experience as a part of his punishment the loss of the ability to hear the truth from God.

It is something of a surprise that in a passage which is in essence the refusal of any prophetic word for people who try to worship both Yahweh and idols, offering simply the reading of the law to them instead, there appear two hopeful elements. For the first time in the book there is a call to repent (vs. 6). Note that it is not accompanied by any promise, only by a warning of what happens to those who do not turn away from idols, but at least it acknowledges that repentance is possible, and the chance to have a different future which is offered by the call to repent will become a prominent part of Ezekiel's message to the exiles eventually (especially chap. 18). And the passage does end with a repetition of the covenant promise, "that they may be my people and I may be their God," as the intended result of the purging from their midst of all idol worshippers. These texts reveal further evidence, then, that the community in exile was an "unfaithful remnant," but in 14:1–11, especially, we can see some clues that the prophet understood God had not given up on them completely, some indications that his work might accomplish more than just convince them that a prophet had been among them (2:5).

Conclusion

Whenever conditions change drastically there are two common temptations which arise, examples of which are contained in this part of the book of Ezekiel. The first is the temptation to stay with the traditional simply because it is tradition, without asking whether it is valid and appropriate for the present needs. This is the result of finding it too painful to subject what we've always done to careful and critical scrutiny, to find out what is worth keeping, what was once valuable but is no longer useful, and what should have been done away with long ago because it was never right. So, there were prophets in exile who continued to offer the traditional messages of *shalom* in a time when God had taken away their *shalom*. They were unable to hear a new word for a new situation, but looked for comfort in what used to be true. Also, the elders continued to try to combine the worship of Yahweh with idolatry, as they had done in Judah, without asking whether Ezekiel might be right when he said the disaster they had just survived was Yahweh's judgment of that.

The second temptation is to look for easy ways to deal with profound problems. The easy way for the prophets was to say what people wanted to hear. To ask their people to be self-critical or to take seriously the possibility of a permanent and drastic change in their lives would not make them very popular, so they looked for easy helps. And some of the women prophets gave in to the temptation to try to manipulate life. This is another easy way, finding some technique to make things go the way you want, rather than facing situations which may require oneself to change. It is too easy, because it doesn't work, but the temptation to manipulate people and things around us still exists and still is little better than magic, even though it now takes on much more sophisticated forms.

Although the specific problems which Ezekiel faced in dealing with the leadership of his community may not reappear in that form in our communities, the essential nature of the temptations which lie behind them is a perennial thing, reappearing especially when significant changes occur, and identifiable in the reactions of contemporary leadership, and perhaps in ourselves as well.

Allegories on Jerusalem's Sin and Fall
(15:1—17:24; 19:1–14; 20:45–49; 23:1—24:14)

"Ah Lord God! they are saying of me, 'Is he not a maker of allegories?' " (20:49). The answer to that rhetorical question is, yes indeed, Ezekiel was the foremost maker of allegories in the Bible. Other prophets used vivid and effective metaphors (see Isa 30:12–14) and occasionally told brief narratives which functioned like parables (for example Isa 5:1–7; Hos 11:1–9), but only Ezekiel takes the traditional prophetic metaphors and spins them out into elaborate, lengthy and detailed stories which have a double meaning. Three times he uses the vine, which was a favorite symbol for Israel, and twice he takes up the theme of the unfaithful wife. The lion, the forest fire, the cooking pot, the merchant ship, and sheep and their shepherds are also used in original ways to represent some truth about Israel and their God. Sometimes he turns them into extended narratives which have no exact parallel elsewhere in the Bible, but elsewhere he more briefly elaborates the metaphor in a way which is relatively common among biblical authors. As we deal with these passages individually we shall begin to see some of the reasons why Ezekiel developed this style and shall consider its effectiveness, then at the conclusion of this section it should be worthwhile to consider what the modern preacher can learn from this prophet's use of language.

This group of seven passages deals with only one subject, the sins and impending fall of Jerusalem. That is a very familiar subject to us by now, so we need not dwell on it at length, even though Ezekiel did. The great variety of ways he developed to talk about the same things shows both the importance and the difficulty of getting the point across to the exiles. Assuming that it is easier for us to understand and accept the truth about the fall of Jerusalem, the discussions of each of these passages will contain two emphases: any spe-

cial aspect of Jerusalem's fate which is highlighted by the
choice of a particular metaphor, and certain important theological contributions which happen to appear in the midst of
the allegory. The central message of the sin and fall of Jerusalem and its broad theological significance have already
been discussed in sections 3, 4, and 5.

This group of passages does not include all the allegories in
the book, but only those concerning the fall of Jerusalem. In
chapter 27 the city of Tyre becomes a merchant ship which
sinks in a storm at sea, and in chapter 34 the people of Israel
and their leaders become sheep and shepherds. Also, in the
oracles against the nations, Ezekiel takes up themes which
were familiar elements in the myths of the ancient Near
East, such as the first man in the garden (chap. 28), the sea
monster (chaps. 29, 32), and the cosmic tree (chap. 31), and
uses them no longer as myth but essentially the same way he
has used other themes to make allegories. So there will be
additional discussion of this literary technique in connection
with those other passages.

The Worthless Vine (15:1–8)

The question at the beginning of this chapter sounds as
though it might have been intended to be a riddle: "How
does the wood of the vine surpass any wood?" But we soon
discover that there is no clever, positive answer to the question; as the rhetorical questions which follow make clear, the
wood of the vine is not superior to other woods in any way
whatsoever. This is a highly unusual, and in fact rather
strange, use of the familiar image of the vine as a symbol for
Israel. Vines are raised for their grapes, and Isaiah and
Jeremiah had already spoken of Israel as a vine which did
not produce as expected (Isa 5:1–7; Jer 2:21), but who would
think of declaring a vine to be useless because its wood cannot be used for anything except fuel? We find no indication of
the reaction of his audience to this, but it is hard to imagine
accepting such a comparison without protest. Who knows?
Maybe that is why Ezekiel did it, to get them drawn into a
discussion of the utter failure of Jerusalem by saying something outrageous. At any rate, his conclusion that vine wood
is good only for burning leads to the prophetic message concerning Jerusalem: It will be consumed by fire.

This chapter is not quite an allegory, in that it doesn't have much of a plot. It is an argumentative use of themes drawn from nature in order to make a point about human affairs, such as we find in Jotham's parable (Judg 9:7–15). But this text and 20:45–49 have been included with the full-fledged allegories because they are also examples of Ezekiel's creative use of imagery, and they have the same subject. In this case, there seems to be a kind of parallel between the inappropriateness of the comparison (judging the wood instead of the fruit) and the unacceptability of the message. He tries to reason with them elsewhere, and with all the questions at the beginning it sounds as though he is reasoning here, but the contents of these verses show that it is really an attack.

The Foundling Child (16:1–63)

The attack on all that the exiles have believed and hoped becomes most severe in this chapter and in chapter 23. Ezekiel claims that the history and the behavior of their beloved city of Jerusalem have been totally without merit. They all knew that the place had been a Canaanite city until relatively late in their history, but they had not emphasized that; rather they had taken heart in the belief that in the time of David God had made a special choice of that city to be his own place. Ezekiel does not deny the divine choice, that is a very important element in the allegory, but he dwells on the complete lack of qualifications to make Jerusalem fit in any way to be called the city of God. His knowledge of the history of the place is accurate when he says her mother was a Hittite and her father an Amorite, but from that point on he becomes theological. The baby was unwanted, unloved, and uncared for, cast out into the field to die. Then Ezekiel combines Hosea's imagery of God as father (or nursemaid?; Hos 11) and God as husband (Hos 2) in order to tell an imaginary life-story of a foundling child whose life is saved by a kindly passerby, who grows up to marry that same benefactor, thus becoming the richest and most elegant of women, but whose sexual drives lead her to total destruction. The use of adultery as a metaphor for the worship of other gods is not new, of course, since it was developed by both Hosea and Jeremiah, but it should be noted that worship, whether of the true God or of idols, is considered by these prophets to be described appropriately in terms of the sexual relationship. We might ask ourselves if that does not make worship a more intimate and a more serious matter for them than it tends to be for most of our contemporaries.

The allegory continues through vs. 34, with occasional lapses into realistic language, as in vss. 17, 20–21, then a prophetic word announces the judgment of the adulterous wife, with a mixture of allegorical and realistic language (vss. 35–43). The rest of the chapter contains two supplements to the basic text, both of which may have been added by Ezekiel himself at a slightly later time. In vss. 44–58 a new element is introduced in the person of two sisters of Jerusalem (somewhat inconsistent with the original foundling theme), the cities of Samaria and Sodom. The point of the comparison which is now made is the worst accusation which has ever been made against Jerusalem, that she is even worse than Sodom, the epitome of wickedness. As if the allegory had not been shocking enough, even worse insults are now heaped upon the "holy city." But the final verses of the chapter contain a promise concerning God's gracious intentions for the future, the re-establishment of the covenant (vss. 59–63). The promise in no way overcomes the effect of the condemnations which have preceded, however, for the gift of the everlasting covenant will have a result which nothing else has produced: Finally they will acknowledge their shame.

Why tell such a gross and highly offensive story? The message behind it is, of course, shocking in its own right and just unacceptable on all grounds. But the story, because it is a story, provides a way to entice people to think about it just because they have a normal desire to see how it comes out, and also because of the elaborate details which attract interest even though one disapproves of what is being said. The chapter is thus an excellent example of how one person developed a technique of getting attention and holding it. More on technique at the end of the section.

Because of its length and its explicitness it is not likely that many sermons are preached from this chapter, but it does in fact contain a very significant contribution to the theology of the book. Here we find one of the Bible's strongest statements about unconditional election based solely on the grace of God. It is God's unmerited favor which links the beginning and end of the passage. Jerusalem is introduced as a found-ling child, destined for death, and only by the free choice of God, without deserving or earning anything, was she given life and every good gift. By her thoroughgoing ungratefulness she forfeits all that, but in the promise which is added at the end, Ezekiel expresses his conviction that for God's own rea-sons, which have nothing to do with anything that she is or has done, restoration will one day become possible. Notice carefully that even repentance *follows* salvation as its result (twice, in vss. 60–61 and 62–63), so thoroughly does Ezekiel speak of salvation by grace alone. This same teaching reap-pears in chapters 20 and 36. So if chap. 16 proves to be too difficult to preach, that important aspect of biblical theol-ogy, which Ezekiel expresses as emphatically as any author in Scripture, can be preached using other passages as the pri-mary texts.

The Cedar and the Eagle (17:1–24)

Two of the chapters which concern us in this section focus on the end of the Davidic monarchy, which will coincide with the fall of Jerusalem. Both of them develop allegories based on the plant world, and chapter 19 also depicts the royal house as a family of lions. Whereas chapters 15 and 16 do not have any special introduction, chapter 17 alerts us that it is a special kind of speech, "a riddle and an allegory" the RSV calls it, although the word translated allegory is not as specific as that. It is also used of proverbs and other kinds of non-literal speech. The story of the eagle, the tree, and the vine, which follows, is a totally unrealistic narrative using elements from the natural world to depict recent and im-pending events in history. Ezekiel's allegories are never meant to be mystifying, and this one could be if a key were not provided, and so the whole thing is explained in vss. 11–21. That does not make the story dispensable, however, for the imagery of the eagle and the cedar twig will be re-membered, like it or not, far more effectively than the recital of facts of history. The allegory tells of the exiling of King Jehoiachin in 597 (vs. 4), the establishment of Zedekiah as vassal king (vss. 5–6), and of his negotiations with Egypt (vs. 7) which would result in his loss of kingship and the end of the monarchy (vss. 9–10). The basis for the judgment of

Zedekiah's efforts as contrary to the will of God is his faithlessness to the oath which he took to Nebuchadnezzar. The oath was sworn in the name of Yahweh and so it counts, the prophet insists, even though it involved the subjugation of his people. Note that the word covenant is used six times and the word oath four times within seven verses, so the emphasis is unmistakable. This time it is not the failure of Judah's kings to maintain justice or to purify the corrupt cult which is cited as the basis for their coming judgment, but taking the name of Yahweh in vain. The move toward breaking his oath to Nebuchadnezzar probably seemed all the more reprehensible to Ezekiel because of the prophet's conviction that subjugation and not liberation was in fact the will of God for Judah in that time.

This is the first significant treatment of the monarchy which we have found in the book, and the message that God was about to cut off the Davidic line, which they believed would be upheld by Yahweh in Jerusalem forever (2 Sam 7; Pss 89; 132), would also have been a very hard idea to accept. Ezekiel deals rather more gently with the kings than he does with Jerusalem, however, perhaps because the one he accepts as the legitimate king, Jehoiachin, is already in exile and not much of a danger to anyone.

As a promise was added to the end of chapter 16, probably some time after the original passage was formulated, here also a promise of the renewal of the monarchy has been appended, probably some time after 587. As is always true of Ezekiel's promises there is a sharp discontinuity between present and future. There is no suggestion in vss. 22–24 that Jehoiachin will regain his throne, but only the promise that some time in the future God himself will take the initiative to appoint a new king from the line of David. That king will be so unlike the former ones that the author finds it appropriate to expand the vegetation imagery in order to bring in the idea of the cosmic tree under which all living things may dwell (more on this in connection with chap. 31).

What is there to preach from this chapter? Both the judgment and the promise remind us of a major OT theme which does not appear with much prominence in the NT, so that Christians have sometimes found it convenient to neglect it. The theme is God's intense interest in government. The OT insists that it makes a difference to God whether people have good government or not, and that lies behind all that is said about kingship in the prophets, historical books, and also the psalms. Ezekiel tends to say less about kingship than the other prophets, and we can understand that because of his peculiar situation, but the concern is not missing from his work, and we find it clearly expressed in chapters 17 and 19, as well as in the promises of 34 and 37.

The Lionness and the Vine (19:1–14)

This chapter contains two allegories dealing with kingship, the first depicting the queen mother as a lionness who has two cubs whose success is brief, the second speaking of mother and son as a vine. The identity of the figures referred to has been debated, since no interpretation has been added by the prophet on this occasion. Since the first lion cub is taken to Egypt and the second to Babylonia one has a point with which to begin, however, for Jehoahaz was the only king to be exiled to Egypt. Also, there was a queen mother who had two sons acceed to the throne, and both of them were exiled. She was Hamutal, one of Josiah's wives (2 Kings 23:31; 24:18). Visualizing the family tree may help to understand the allegory:

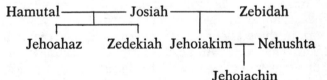

Although there are other theories, it seems most probable that the three characters in vss. 1–9 are Hamutal, Jehoahaz, and Zedekiah, and that vss. 10–14 deal with Hamutal and Zedekiah. The end of the monarchy as represented by the exiling of two members of the family of David is the subject of both allegories, then, but what is most important to us theologically, in this chapter, is the title which is given to them. They are called lamentations—more accurately, funeral songs, and that adds something to what has by now become a very familiar message. Ezekiel does not gloat because those inept kings get what is coming to them; the whole thing is a tragedy, from God's point of view, and his prophet laments the end of the rule of that family which should have produced righteous kings.

The Forest Fire (20:45–49)

As we picture modern Israel an immense forest fire seems a very strange image for any prophet to choose, especially when our translations contain the word Negev, which usually refers to the area south of Beersheba where almost nothing but grass grows. But *negev* here probably simply means "south," which is its meaning as a common noun, since there has never in historic times been any forest land in the Negev. Since the exiles would have traveled north through Syria when they left their homes to begin the journey to Babylonia, commentators suggest that Ezekiel's use of the direction south here simply refers to Palestine. Others also remind us of the enemy from the north, of which Jeremiah speaks (1:13–15) and which reappears in Ezek 38–39, as a possible background for speaking of a fire sweeping down toward the south. As for the forest, it is known that the hills of Palestine were covered with trees in antiquity and that the barrenness of the country today is the result of centuries of human occupation. This short text is no more a true allegory than chapter 15 is, since neither has a plot, but it represents a vivid use of imagery, for it is clearly no real fire of which Ezekiel speaks, but the judgment of the Lord. Probably the most important thing about this text is the audience reaction which he attaches to it. "Ah Lord God they are saying of me, 'Is he not a maker of allegories?'" It suggests to us that despite the skill with which he devised new methods of communication, it was still possible to disbelieve, indeed to hear and remember the stories but go no further than to accept them as well-told stories (see 33:30–32). The sentence stands, then, as another bit of evidence concerning the nature of his audience and the magnitude of his task.

The Unfaithful Sisters (23:1–49)

The theme of the unfaithful wife reappears in this chapter, developed with a coarseness of language which can scarcely be paralleled elsewhere in the Bible. It is a good example of the reasons why one should never go too far in finding meaning in the details of an allegory, for in this story God has two wives and both of them had been harlots in Egypt before he married them. Unlike chapter 16, which tells us something about the character of God, this chapter really speaks only of the character of the two sisters. The foundling child in the earlier chapter began life merely as an unfortunate person, but in 23 the emphasis is on the degenerate nature of Oholah and Oholibah from the beginning: "They played the harlot in Egypt" (vss. 3, 8, 19–21). This is one of Ezekiel's total depravity chapters and its shocking suggestion that God chose two harlots to become his wives is at bottom not so very different from the theology of Romans 5:6–10: "Christ died for the ungodly ... while we were yet sinners Christ died for us ... while we were enemies we were reconciled to God. ..."

Although the harlotry in chap. 16 may refer to the worship of other gods, as it does in Hosea and Jeremiah, it should be noted that in this chapter it has a specifically political reference. It is the efforts of Samaria and Jerusalem to determine their own destinies by negotiations with Assyria and Babylonia, which involve giving up their intended uniqueness as the people of Yahweh, which Ezekiel dwells on in this allegory of their history. In this chapter, then, he reminds us a bit of the concerns of Isaiah, who focused so intently on the relationship between politics and the Yahwistic faith.

As for preaching the message of this passage, it will probably be very hard to make this story a meaningful one for a contemporary congregation, but we might let Eichrodt's comment on chapter 16 become a useful suggestion, for it applies equally well to this chapter. He says the story portrays "what a revoltingly ugly thing it is" to be unfaithful, and it may be that when the time comes that we need to say something about unfaithfulness, an effective way to do it would be, not to expound the details of Ezek 16 or 23, but to let that prophet's skill in storytelling guide us toward saying the same kind of thing in terms of a contemporary story.

The Corroded Cauldron (24:1–14)

This last allegory concerning the fall of Jerusalem is given special weight by the date which is attached to it, marking it as having been uttered on the very day when Nebuchadnezzar laid siege to Jerusalem. It is a complex if not contorted use of imagery, reminiscent of chapter 15 in its surprising

turns. It is identified as an allegory (or comparative or figur-
ative saying, as mentioned in connection with 17:2), but
sounds like the instructions for a symbolic act at the beginning—except that the instructions seem to be directed toward the exiles rather than to Ezekiel. The reasons for the
imperatives in vss. 3–5 have been explained quite satisfacto-
rily by the suggestion that this is a quotation or adaptation
of a work song, the kind of chant that might have been used
by cooks as they prepared a feast. It now becomes the apparently innocuous introduction to an allegory which, like chapter 15, picks up something completely unexpected and
develops it in a highly original way. Since the work song
might have reminded Ezekiel's listeners of the saying quoted
from the leaders of Jerusalem in 11:3, they might have expected him to comment on it somewhat the way he had already done earlier. This time, however, he informs them that
the kettle itself is heavily corroded and the treatment of that
utensil becomes the main subject. (It is more likely to have
been copper or an alloy thereof than iron, so the term corro-
sion is to be preferred to rust.) He tells us immediately that
the cauldron represents Jerusalem, labeled as in chapter 22
the bloody city. Its contents are to be cooked, all right, but
then the corroded pot is to be set back on the heaped up fire
so as to melt it down. It has flaws in it which are so serious
that nothing but remelting and starting over will solve the
problem. Nothing else has helped (vs. 13). So Ezekiel has
found another way to speak of the thoroughness of that end
which he believes is about to come upon the beloved city. In
the conclusion he puts it in ponderously plain words:

> I the Lord have spoken;   it shall come to pass
> I will do it;   I will not go back;
> I will not spare,   I will not repent;
> according to your ways and your doings I will judge
> you, says the Lord God.

Conclusions

The allegories emphasize the desperateness of Jerusalem's
situation more than anything else Ezekiel did. She is as useless as the wood of a grape vine or a hopelessly corroded pot
and like both she is destined for the fire. She is as pure and

trustworthy as a woman who chases after every man she meets; she is the worst city in the world, worse than Sodom. Surely it must have been for shock effect that the prophet composed these appalling stories. Note the contrast between the allegories concerning Jerusalem and those which deal with the monarchy. The latter use symbols of nobility drawn from nature, cedars, lions, and vines, and do not pervert them, the way all the symbols used for Jerusalem are twisted. Obviously the house of David is not the big stumbling block which Ezekiel needs to deal with, and so its downfall is described with overtones of lamentation as well as judgment. But the inability of Jerusalem to stand, before Yahweh as well as before Nebuchadnezzar, is the unacceptable message which Ezekiel tries his best to get across, using every means imaginable. We shall encounter yet one more effort, the retelling of salvation history, in chapter 20.

The central message of these allegories is extremely important for OT theology, for reasons explained in the introduction (and see also the comments on chap. 37), and its close relationship with the NT's theology of the cross makes it a subject which should not be neglected by us, but certainly we do not need to preach the theological significance of the fall of Jerusalem as often as Ezekiel did. This means there is more material on the subject in chapters 1—24 of this book than most preachers can ever use. But it may be that Ezekiel's technique can be helpful to the preacher, even though some of these passages are never used as texts for sermons. We can learn something from his insistence on trying new ways to get a message across. He knew all the traditional ways, but knew also that it was a totally new situation and that he had a message which was going to be hard for anyone to believe, and so we can see in him a creativity which we do well to emulate. Why make up these elaborate allegories? Why not just say it straight? If you are familiar with the recent literature on homiletics, you will recognize that storytelling is the subject of more than one of the books which are attempting to persuade preachers to look for more effective ways of getting their message across than the traditional three or five points of doctrine or ethical teaching. In other words the modern literature suggests that we try to discover how to do what Ezekiel already discovered in the sixth century B.C. The good story not only helps to get people's attention and keep it, but there is also the possibility of persuasive power in pictorial language, which may by its imagery plant an idea in the mind even when the intellect resists and resents it. So Israel remembered the foundling child even though they found the idea outrageous and could not, at first, believe the implications of the imagery.

Please note, however, that not every sermon was an allegory. There are more ways to convey the truth than storytelling, and for those why may become overly enthusiastic about it, Ezekiel's reminder that variety is essential may also be needed.

The Past Is Not Irrevocable
(Ezekiel 18:1–32; 33:10–20)

This chapter clearly represents a part of Ezekiel's work in building the new community in exile, and so there is some question about whether it should be dated before 587 B.C., as its location in the book suggests, or whether the brief parallel in 33:10–20 is an accurate pointer to its correct date, in the later part of his ministry. At any rate, it needs to be understood that the message of the chapter is constructive and has a very different aim from those around it. We encounter here one of the key pastoral issues which faced Ezekiel, the question which we label "theodicy."

It appears that the question of whether God is just, and if he is, how his justice can be defended, became a critical issue at just about this time in the history of Israel. It is the subject of Habakkuk (dated about 600 B.C.), aspects of the problem appear in the so-called Confessions of Jeremiah (see Jer 12:1), and there are reasons for thinking the book of Job may also have originated in its present form at about this time. The faith of Israel encountered an unprecedented challenge in these years. All they had believed in was being taken away. Did it mean they were wrong about God himself? Many of the exiles appear to have drawn that conclusion. There's no justice in this world, they complained. "The fathers have eaten sour grapes, and the children's teeth are set on edge." Sure, we know our ancestors did a lot of rotten things, but why should *we* have to suffer for it? What have *we* done to deserve this? It isn't fair! Ezekiel finds himself facing a cynicism so prevalent that it has taken the form of a mocking proverb.

He does not discuss the whole subject of theodicy. As Gerhard von Rad says, there is here "no theoretical sketch of a universally valid doctrine of the righteousness of Yahweh and Israel." He works as a pastor and responds to the particular problem raised by his people at that time, with an answer which he hopes will meet that specific need. He doesn't discuss presuppositions or corollaries; he is talking to people who hurt, and offering medicine for that hurt. Theodicy is a complex philosophical and theological question, but it is fundamentally a pastoral problem.

Although Ezekiel does not discuss presuppositions, we need to be sure we understand what they were. The term we have invented to help us understand the outlook of the ancient Israelite on identity is "corporate personality." This is our effort to describe the way they seemed to think of their identity first in terms of the group to which they belonged, and then only secondarily as individuals. The form in which that self-understanding appears in this chapter may be called "corporate responsibility." As examples of that, consider Achan (Josh 7), whose children were executed along with him because he stole some of the treasure from Jericho; and Naboth (1 Kings 21), who refused to sell his vineyard because he understood himself to be holding it in trust for his descendants. As ancient Israel saw it, one's identity and also one's guilt or righteousness were not compartmentalized so that they have no effect on others. Those who were closest, families, shared a common character and a common fate. This is not a presupposition of ours and we find aspects of it to be shocking, improper, and untrue, but there is some truth in the Israelite outlook, whether we like it or not. Children do suffer for the sins and benefit from the righteousness of their ancestors. One person's righteous deed can bring blessings to many who have done nothing to deserve them, and one person's sin can bring suffering to many who bear no blame for it. Our destinies are bound up together to a far greater extent than our individualistic outlook is ready to admit.

There had been many disruptions and exceptions to the Israelite outlook, but until the time of the exile, corporate responsibility was the generally accepted point of view. People lived for the most part in stable communities, in the same houses where their ancestors had lived, next to the same neighbors, farming the same fields, and they were buried in the same family tombs. But now all that was changed. Families had been broken up, houses and land and neighbors were lost forever. Beginning with Jeremiah and Ezekiel we find theological reflections of the rise of individualism which challenged the old assumptions about life, and which must have been virtually unavoidable, under the circumstances.

Such a challenge appears in that proverb which Ezekiel quotes, which in the old days might have been a simple statement of fact. Sons do suffer for the sins of their fathers. But that is not how the exiles mean it. Later in the chapter the prophet quotes them again: "Yet you say, 'The way of the Lord is not just.' " They are quoting the proverb because they want to ask, *Why* must the sons suffer for the sins of the father? It isn't right, they are complaining. Ezekiel offers a defense of God in response to this, but what is more important, he also offers a promise.

Each Generation is Responsible for Itself (18:1–20)

He is a priest, trained in the law, and his answer is a series of cases, making use of sacral law in the traditional wording of priestly responses. But he will do something original with it. He begins with a basic case (vss. 5–9), from which he will move to a whole series of variations, quoting the law and concluding with the statement by which the priests declared a person to be fit to enter and participate in the cultic community: "He is righteous, he shall surely live." There is actually nothing new in any of this. The sins which are mentioned he quotes from the law, and the declaration at the end of the paragraph has been shown by recent studies to be the standard language used by the priest to declare that a person was fit to join in the worship of the community. As a prophet Ezekiel is here using the priestly language which he had learned from his family's vocation. "Righteous" in this context thus means one who has met the basic requirements of harmonious relationship, a sampling of which Ezekiel has quoted. And "he shall surely live" does not refer to escaping the death penalty, and certainly not to eternal life, which is not an idea discussed at all in Israel at this time, but to life in the worshipping community as it drew near to the source of life, Yahweh.

Two additional notes on this opening statement: This is no random selection of laws, no standard case out of the tradition which his audience could easily divorce themselves from, for elsewhere Ezekiel has accused his own generation of precisely the same sins. All but one of the sins cited here appear elsewhere as parts of the prophet's specific condemnation of the factors which are bringing about the fall of Jerusalem (see especially chap. 22). This is *your* problem, and no one else's, Ezekiel is saying. The other point to note is that the laws he quotes had always been individualistic. None of them calls for punishments of anyone but the single person guilty of the misdeed. This chapter is not dealing with some brand new idea of individual responsibility, for that had always existed in Israel along with the corporate sense, but it represents a new emphasis on individualism.

After this first, basic case, which presumably everyone would recognize and agree with, Ezekiel presents two more, hypothetical generations; the righteous man has a wicked son and a righteous grandson (vs. 10–18). With vs. 17 we get closer to his real point. "He shall not die for his father's iniquity; he shall surely live." This was not new, either, for by Ezekiel's time Israelite law already decreed that children were not to be punished for the sins of their parents (Deut 24:16), but the prophet has made a new application of this principle. Recent studies of this chapter have shown that there are two different issues here. One is criminal responsibility; punishment for disobeying the law. That is not what his audience was talking about. Their issue was divine retribution; the idea that God sends misfortune upon those who rebel against him, but Ezekiel has taken the generally accepted compartmentalization of generations as practiced in the law courts and used it as a response to their complaint about retribution. That explains their otherwise strange and contrary-sounding response to his series of cases: "Yet you say, 'Why should not the son suffer for the iniquity of the father?' " (vs. 19). Now they seem to be arguing *for* corporate responsibility, whereas the whole thing began with their complaints about the injustice of it. But now we see what the real problem is. This is no abstract discussion about the nature and attributes of God. The real issue is the exiles' need to avoid admitting responsibility for the mess they're in. In Ezekiel's hypothetical family tree they *want* the son to suffer for the sins of the father, because they want to argue that is what is happening to them. It's not our fault, they claim, but somebody else's. They are not really complaining about the sour grapes principle; in fact they have a vested interest in its truth, for it lets them off and puts the blame on God. But

Ezekiel finds a way to attack that attitude by isolating the generations, exactly as it was in fact already done in their law, and then by extending the argument from the law court to the fate of whole groups of people such as the community in which he lives (vs. 20).

But now we may find ourselves tempted to join in on the side of the congregation and argue with Ezekiel ourselves. Because in reality it *isn't* all that neat and straightforward. Can or should I say that I have not benefitted in any way from my mother's and father's righteousness? The fact is, I have. And surely we cannot deny that this generation is suffering from the sins of the generations which have gone before us! Ezekiel's extreme and complete compartmentalization of the generations simply does not reflect the world we know. What, then, do we make of such an argument?

The explanation is to be found by asking why the prophet tries to make such a point—that each generation is responsible for its own sins. If we try to make of it a theoretical treatment of sin and guilt, we will find ourselves in deep trouble, for it will not correspond to the rest of Scripture or to life as we know it. The answer is to be found in the emphasis on Ezekiel's work as a pastor. The whole point of this is to try to get a specific group of people to change their minds about something. These are people feeling very sorry about themselves, denying all responsibility for the terrible things that have happened to them. Ezekiel is trying to break through that protective shell, to try to get them to think in new terms about where they stand, to get them just to consider whether they are really as good as they claim.

The whole point of this first half of the chapter is to persuade his congregation that what their ancestors did has not left them helpless and hopeless. They have a chance.

It was easy for them to wallow in bitterness and self-pity as long as they felt sure they could blame their troubles on someone else, and they had found the culprits in the ancestors, and ultimately in God. So the first part of the argument is to get them to consider themselves; to apply the priestly and prophetic standards to their own lives. Ezekiel challenges them with this possibility: No matter how bad your ancestors may have been, *you* could do right, and it would make a difference. Notice that he doesn't fall into that trap of saying, "If you do this, God will reward you with that." He knows it doesn't always work out that way. He offers only the traditional form of acceptance: He shall surely live.

Ezekiel's argument would never hold up in a modern theology textbook. It is an *ad hominem* argument, the work of a pastor, not a theologian, a response to a specific human problem which confronts him in the form of people with faces and voices who need to have their mind changed. He devises an attack on their complacency intended to get them to think, and if it succeeded in doing that, then it was a good argument. It must have had some success, because it's in the Book today. The chapter may be compared in some respects with the teaching which Paul offers in response to specific issues—valid for that immediate situation, but not necessarily to be taken as propositional theology, valid for all times and places. Certainly it is based on an understanding of God and human relationships to God which is valid for all times and places, but the details of the argument are another matter.

Change Is Possible (18:21–32)

This is only the first step toward the prophet's real goal. To convince this people they were only getting what they deserved would hardly in itself produce a strong and vital congregation; it would more likely leave them with a hopeless sense of despair. So a new series of cases is introduced.

He now talks about a single life; about an individual who changes his ways—and that is what he is really aiming for; to get individuals to change their ways. "But if a wicked man turns away from all his sins which he has committed and keeps all my statutes and does what is lawful and right, he shall surely live; he shall not die" (vs. 21). Note that he begins with the wicked man who repents, not with the righteous man who goes wrong, and the reason is that his real message does not concern backsliding, but the possibility of repentance. He emphasizes that in the next sentence: "None of the transgressions which he has committed shall be remembered against him; for the righteousness which he has done he shall live" (vs. 22). Next the legal flavor of the language disappears completely, for he has reached the point of the whole message. Here is the truth which is valid for all times and all places: "Have I any pleasure in the death of the wicked, says the Lord God, and not rather that he should turn from his way and live?" (vs. 23). Change is possible; no one is locked in by what others have done or even by the previous direction of one's own life. And it can go either way, as Ezekiel admits in the next paragraph (vss. 24–25); it may also be that a man who has maintained his righteousness, that is, has decided by his actions in favor of God and has thus been able to participate with the community in a harmonious relationship—such a person may change and become impossible to live with in peace. We know that is so, and sorrow over it, but it is true and Ezekiel knew it.

But those are options that are alive and open to everyone. God is not to be blamed for those failures; they are human choices and they could be avoided. Still, the exiles were looking for excuses, as vs. 25 shows, and God's answer to that is rather blunt: "Is my way not just? . . . Is it not your ways that are not just? . . . Therefore I will judge you, O house of Israel, every one according to his ways, says the Lord God" (vss. 25, 30). Not according to what anyone else has done; here is the individualism they presumably were calling for in their initial complaint—but it has left them without any more excuses. It must be emphasized that this is not Ezekiel's main point, however, for here we come to his gospel. He has tried to find ways to beat down their excuses and get them to admit some responsibility for their own destinies. Why? What good would that do? In part it is to justify God, to maintain a theological foundation for his teaching which preserves the essential truths: God is good and God is in charge. But to justify God by laying the responsibility on the congregation is not enough. The real message he wants to get across is that the future is still open for them.

The past is not irrevocable.

That is the truly revolutionary message for the exiles. Had not their recent past changed everything? Hadn't it done worse than mortgage the future; wasn't it completely lost? Ezekiel's answer is, by no means! What your ancestors did has not shut off your future. You know that the son of a wicked man can choose to live the righteous life. And it is just as true that a person who has lived a wicked life can change radically, and the past does not determine the future.

So the message for the bitter, who shunned the appeal to make something of the opportunities which might just be present in this new place if they could find it in themselves to accept the challenge, is called out in the most urgent way in vss. 30b–32. "Repent and turn from all your transgressions. . . . Why will you die? . . . For I have no pleasure in the death of any one, says the Lord God; so turn, and live."

Even this can be protested, however, if we set ourselves on the side of the cynics who first heard those words. How can he say the past is not irrevocable? For example, we know very well that it is possible to mistreat our bodies to the extent that health can never be restored, even if we do change our lifestyles. The past does *not* completely go away. We know that it is possible to hurt other people so deeply that no matter what we may later do to remedy matters, even if reconciliation is achieved, the pain will never go away, as long as consciousness remains. We know very well that forgiveness, between human beings or between God and human beings, may restore the broken relationship, but does not erase all the suffering the sin has caused.

For the people in our congregations, however, who do not really believe that any significant change is possible in their lives, there is gospel in this chapter. The preacher's task is to get them to move beyond those objections based on the obvious irrevocability of certain aspects of our past (If we've had a leg amputated, that isn't going to get better!) and to encourage them to try to believe that fantastic, indeed miraculous changes are nevertheless possible when the power of God comes into our lives. This chapter is an appeal for repentance, and so it contains language which sounds like "self-help," near the end. "Get yourselves a new heart and a new spirit!" (vs. 31). That is itself not good news to anyone, for how can we, purely by our own efforts, completely change who we are? The answer, of course, is that Ezekiel knew it would have to be God who would make such a transformation, and he promises that will come some day (36:26). In the meantime, there is something we can do, for true repentance is possible and that means our future can be better.

Ezekiel cannot speak of the cross of Christ, but his theology is fully in keeping with that of the NT at this point. The message of his book as a whole teaches that we are saved by grace alone, but just as the NT understands that repentance is an essential part of the acceptance of God's gift to us in Jesus Christ, and an ongoing part of living by faith, so Ezekiel challenges those whose faith is almost gone to try again, and adds to the challenge a promise. "Why will you die, O house of Israel? For I have no pleasure in the death of any one, says the Lord God; so turn, and live." This is the last word, the one undebatable certainty supporting all of Ezekiel's reasonings and pleadings and admonitions. It is the unshakeable intention of God to forgive. Yahweh is the God of life, not of death, and the intention to give life overshadows everything else. Questions of what is just and what is not, of how it might be possible to transcend the crippling effects of the past begin to fade away before the power of that final appeal.

History, Past And Future
(Ezekiel 20:1–44)

The date of this chapter shows that it comes early in Ezekiel's ministry, about two years after his call, and the setting, with certain of the elders of Israel coming to inquire of him, shows that he was to some extent accepted as a prophet to the exilic community. But as in chapter 14, which describes the same setting, Ezekiel was not simply available for consultation on any subject, for in both chapters the message given to the elders is that Yahweh refuses to answer their request, and the reasons for the refusal are spelled out in considerable detail. In neither chapter is the original request even identified for us. Two suggestions have been made. The first is that they were asking the prophet's permission to establish a sacrificial cult in exile (supported by vss. 30–32,40), and the other is that they were asking for the kind of message the other prophets in exile were giving (chap. 13), a word concerning when they would be able to return to the Promised Land. We shall never know if either of these was the actual request, but it is clear that the implied answer to either of them was negative.

The chapter is clearly divided into two parts, and the second part can also be sub-divided. The first (vss. 1–31) is a retelling of the classical period of Israel's history, the second speaks of the future as a time of purging in the wilderness (vss. 32–39) which will be followed by restoration to the land (vss. 40–44). There have been questions about the unity of the chapter but a good case has been made for ascribing all of it except for minor additions to Ezekiel himself. Whether he produced the whole thing at the same time or whether it makes better sense to think of the latter section as an addition which he made to his words of judgment at a later time is still a debated question, but it is not likely to have much effect on the way one deals with the chapter homiletically. They are not two separate units, for the second part refers again and again to the themes of the first, describing the future as God's reversal of the past, so it cannot be dealt with in isolation. Since the first part speaks of complete rejection it is only the presence of the additional words, revealing the possibility of a future in the plan of God, which makes the judgment part preachable.

A series of important themes appears in the chapter, and some of them are developed in a way quite distinctive to Ezekiel. This makes it a highly important chapter in the book. He tries a new form of communication here; the re-telling of the salvation history which was the foundation of the Yahwistic faith. It is used in two original ways, first, by selecting the memories of Israel's rebelliousness which the traditions had preserved, so as to make that the dominant recollection of the past, and then, by projecting the past into the future, affirming that God intends to act once again as he has done before. The retelling in the first part thus brings to the fore three themes: rebellion on Israel's part, amazing patience on God's part, and (no surprise to us by now) the inevitability of judgment. The second part emphasizes the divine motive for salvation—"for my name's sake, not according to your evil ways"—and introduces a new idea which mediates between the threats of almost total annihilation and the unconditional promises of restoration. The new idea is a time of purging in the future which will prepare the exiles for the promised new life.

A History of Continual Rebellion (20:1–31)

Ezekiel's retelling of the classical period of Israel's history, that is, the events from the time of the oppression in Egypt to the occupation of the land of Canaan, is very carefully organized so as to emphasize throughout two of the themes which have just been mentioned, Israel's rebellion and Yahweh's patience. The structure is so important that an outline should be offered to supplement the limited discussions which you may find in the commentaries. It deals with history in a rather static way, with reference to places rather than events, and it unfolds in three stages: the time in Egypt, the first generation in the Wilderness, and the second generation in the Wilderness. The concluding reference to Canaan is tacked on in a rather suspicious way and may not have been part of Ezekiel's original work. Here is the pattern:

	Egypt	First Wilderness Generation	Second Wilderness Generation
God's act of grace	5–6	10	17
His requirement of them	7	11–12	18–20
Their unfaithfulness	8a	13a	21a
God's resolve to punish	8b	13b	21b
Reprieve	9	14	22
But some punishment was threatened		15–16	23–24
And some punishment was exacted			25–26

The material was known to everyone, so Ezekiel could omit the details of the Exodus, wandering in the wilderness and Conquest, and could emphasize the provisions which God made in order that these people might have life, namely the prohibition of idolatry, the observance of his statutes and ordinances, and the celebration of the Sabbath day. What movement there is in the passage involves the tension between God's determination to remain faithful to his promises to Israel, since his honor is involved with those promises, and the need to be just in dealing with a people who have behaved as though they wanted no part of him. He bore with them in Egypt, not punishing them even though they did not fulfill his negative requirement concerning idolatry. (This view is original with Ezekiel, as far as we know, since the book of Exodus says nothing about idolatry (compare Exod 6:9 with Josh 24:14). In the wilderness, however, some punishment must be forthcoming, despite God's faithfulness, probably because at Sinai the people had taken upon themselves a relationship to God which involved questions of justice, as well as grace (vss. 15–16). The promise of the land was not abrogated, but the first generation did not receive it. The second generation repeated the rebellion of the first, so also stood under judgment, but as Ezekiel tells it he cannot deny that they occupied the land, for they did. Instead he simply does not mention the Conquest and puts in its place a threat of exile (vss. 23–24), which would have special poignancy for his audience, among whom it had come true. The punishment of the second generation is described in vss. 25–26, which are the most difficult part of the whole book, if not of the whole Bible.

All the standard translations of vss. 25–26 involve some interpretation, so they should be used with great caution. Literally, this is what the Hebrew says:

> Also I gave them statutes which were not good
> and ordinances by which they could not live,
> And I defiled them by their gifts,
> by offering everything that opens the womb,
> so that I might stupefy them,
> in order that they might know that I am Yahweh.

No where else in the Bible does it say that God gave laws that were not good; even Paul is not so radical as this (see Rom 7:7–12). If that were not bad enough, the next line is generally taken to be a reference to child-sacrifice, and that is associated with the action of God, as well. These statements are made about the second generation in the wilderness, and there is nothing anywhere else in the biblical tradition which corresponds to them. Thus, it is likely that Ezekiel intended them to be a description of the entire history of Israel, from the time of its occupation of Canaan to the present. It is an exact reversal of the conditions which God established for Israel's life with him. They were not to defile themselves (vss. 7b, 18b), but now he will defile them; they could find life by keeping his statutes and ordinances (vss. 11, 13, 21), but now he gives them laws which do not provide life. It is suggested that these terrible verses are a message to the exiles analogous to the word that Yahweh had abandoned the temple and was committing Jerusalem over to destruction. Here Ezekiel says Yahweh has abandoned the sacrificial cult, which had been intended as a means of access to him—thus to life—but which is in fact now invalid. If this is a correct interpretation of these verses, it would support the suggestion that the elders had come asking for prophetic help in establishing a sacrificial cult in Babylonia. His indirect answer would be in line with the condemnations of the cult in other prophetic books; that is, God does not accept the gifts of unrepentant people (see Isa 1:10–17).

This interpretation of vss. 25–26 is slightly different from what you will find in any of the commentaries and calls for a detailed argumentation which cannot be provided here, but the reasons for it can be summarized briefly. Ezekiel refers to two aspects of the sacrificial cult: "gifts" and "offering up everything that opens the womb," that is, every first-born. No one has bothered to discuss the first term, because it is so bland and seems a perfectly innocent word except for its use on occasion in the wisdom literature, where it can denote a bribe. The second has been regularly taken as a clear reference to child-sacrifice, in part because of the verb which is used, but largely one may suspect, because that practice is explicitly mentioned in vs. 31. The expression "everything that opens the womb" is never used elsewhere of human sacrifice, however, and is actually an exact quotation of the law in Exod 13:12, which specifies the offering of every first-born to God *except* of asses and human beings, which are to be redeemed. Ezekiel's sentence is thus a verbal reference to a perfectly legitimate law which provided for the sacrifice of the first-born, but specifically excluded human sacrifice. It is a law which is subject to perversion, however, by those who do not fully understand or are willing to make compromises with the Yahwistic faith, as the examples of child sacrifice mentioned in the OT reveal to us (see 2 Kings 16:3; 21:6; 23:10). But the argument here is that Ezekiel has referred to two, originally legitimate provisions of the divine law, by which Israel might have lived, and has chosen these two on purpose because they were particularly susceptible to human perversion once they were no longer signs of God's grace. The law of the first-born, when misunderstood by men such as Ahaz and Manasseh to call for a human sacrifice, becomes a horrible example of what happens to people whom Yahweh has deserted, and the "gifts" of those whom Yahweh no longer looks upon with favor became nothing more than ineffectual attempts at bribery.

The suggestion is that these are not new laws, given to the second generation in the wilderness or to Israel in Canaan, but that the word "give" is used in a broader sense (as it often is, in Hebrew) to refer to what God has made of the laws promulgated at Sinai. The term "not good" would then mean in this context, "useless" or "invalid," and the effect of vs. 25 would be to say that God made his laws (which were originally life-giving) invalid, because of the perennial rebellion of Israel, so that they could no longer have access to God through them. Instead, those very laws which had been intended as blessings now defile them, through perversions of their original meaning, as illustrated by the laws of gifts and the first-born. Such an explanation may alleviate some of the scandal associated with the text, in that it downplays human sacrifice, but these verses still remain one of the severest messages in the Bible, for they say to the exiles that what we would call "the means of grace" are no longer available to them.

Yes, the passage contains an important message about God's patience, but its conclusion contains a terrifying warning that there are limits even to the patience of God.

"Future History" (20:32–44)

It has been suggested that the saying quoted in vs. 32, "Let us be like the nations, like the tribes of the countries, and worship wood and stone" (probably something Ezekiel attributes to them rather than something the elders actually said), is an indication that they were proposing to set up a sacrificial cult to Yahweh in exile, and if so, the interpretation just given of vss. 25–26 would deflate those pretensions very effectively, since it would say to them that the sacrificial cult of Yahweh is no longer effective. This transitional verse, affirming that their desire to be like the nations in this respect will never happen, then leads to the message of God's intention for the future of the exiles, expressed in two parts. The first (vss. 33–39) makes use of elements from the classical history, the stories of rebellion and chastisement in the wilderness, to provide a pattern which is now projected into the future. "Wilderness," which might be the actual desert separating them from Palestine or might also be used symbolically of the exile experience, is to be a place of purging for all who have been dispersed from the Promised Land. Now, finally, the sorting out of the faithful from the syncretists will take place (vss. 37–39), so that a true congregation of Yahweh will come into existence. It has not happened yet, but Ezekiel promises it is coming.

Only then will sacrifice again be acceptable, as the second part of this picture of the future indicates (vs. 40). Once again, passing through the wilderness will lead to the Promised Land (vss. 41–42), and in that land, on God's holy mountain, their offerings will once again be acceptable. This is one of Ezekiel's few favorable references to Jerusalem (outside of

chaps. 40–48), and it is significant that he neither uses the
name of the city nor the title Zion, since both of them carry
too many connotations which he has been arguing against.
Of course Jerusalem as it is now cannot be saved, and no
early or easy return of the exiles to that place is suggested.
They exist now without the means of access to God which
sacrificial worship had provided, and only after a purging
process has removed from the exilic community those who
still refuse to understand and obey will the fullness of life
with their God once again be possible.

Two important aspects of Ezekiel's theology appear in this
passage. As in 16:59-63, the initiative toward restoration is
entirely God's. Even repentance is the result, not the cause of
the change. Note that it is after God has purged and restored
them to the land that they finally remember their ways and
loathe themselves for all the evils which they have committed. The same order will be found also in 36:31, and it corresponds to the truth of at least some people's Christian
experience. It happens that we truly despise what we have
done only when we realize that we have been forgiven for it
and are willing to accept that forgiveness, for until we can
accept forgiveness we need to go on defending ourselves and
refusing to acknowledge sin as it really is. Evidently there is
another kind of experience as well, encountered by those who
feel themselves oppressed under the burden of their sins and
filled with the need to find a way to be freed from them
which at last they hear in the message of divine forgiveness,
the promise of freedom which they have been seeking. But
there are many whose sins are not so obvious, at least to
themselves, who don't really know and are by no means
ready to acknowledge that they are sinners in desperate need
of forgiveness until they understand the cross. Only then
does it become possible to admit how wrong they have been,
when they know that forgiveness is possible, even for that.
There are a great many, essentially decent people who fit
that category, and Ezekiel is talking about all those who
don't even think they have anything significant to repent of
until they realize that grace has been at work on their behalf
long before they knew they needed it.

Ezekiel does not use the words "grace" or "love" of God;
his language is harsh even when his subject is mercy (and

that word is used only in 39:25). But we should not be put off by the language, for Ezekiel's concept of God points directly toward the NT. The people are hopeless, as he has analyzed things, and there is no humanly calculable future to be seen in Jerusalem or in exile. But God has the power to do anything he wills, and so the real question is what God wills to do. Ezekiel's gospel is, "when I deal with you for my name's sake, not according to your evil ways" (vs. 44). The prophet has learned that Yahweh is determined to create a people after his own heart, come what may, and he assures his people that there is nothing which anyone can do which will ultimately thwart his will. In his "name," that is, in the divine character there is something which overrides all human obstacles in his will to save. So the chapter which began with a reminder of the patience of God in spite of that perennial human rebellion which eventually had to be dealt with, concludes appropriately with the assurance that their well-deserved sufferings are not the end of the story, for God's final intention is salvation.

The Nations
(Ezekiel 25:1—32:32; 35:1–15)

In this carefully organized book, most of the work which Ezekiel did before the fall of Jerusalem in 587 has been gathered into chapters 1—24, and everything from chapter 33 to the end clearly is to be dated after that event. In the middle of the book, then, bracketed by the divine announcement to Ezekiel that Nebuchadnezzar had laid siege to the city (24:2) and the arrival of a messenger in Babylonia with the news of its fall (33:21), there appears a collection of oracles against foreign nations. They are carefully dated (in fact, seven of the thirteen dates in the book are in chaps. 25—32), so we can see that most of them are located in about the right place, chronologically, for six of the dates fall between 587 and 585. The seventh is far out of place, for it bears the latest date of any passage in the book (571 B.C.; 29:17–20), but the reason for its presence here is obvious; it deals with Tyre and Egypt and has been grouped with other oracles dealing with those places on a topical principle of arrangement. According to the dates and the structure of the book, then, Ezekiel took a special interest in the destinies of Tyre and Egypt (adding brief oracles about other nations) during the siege of Jerusalem and just afterward. The reasons are not hard to find. Egypt had been an enticement to poor political decisions in Judah on many occasions, since from its perspective Palestine was a buffer zone to protect it from invasions from the north. More than once it had offered help to Judah which it failed to deliver, and that very thing happened during the last siege (Jer 37:5). Ezekiel needed to talk about Egypt, then, since for the exiles it was one of the sources of hope which would soon fail them. Tyre provided a different basis for hope. It was built on an island just off the Phoenician coast, meaning that the usual forms of siege-craft were of no avail against it. Nebuchadnezzar's army camped on the shore opposite the island for thirteen years, until it finally surrendered in 571, and the occasional piece of news which may have come to the exiles indicating that Tyre was still holding out may have encouraged them to think that successful resistance to Nebuchadnezzar was possible after all.

The purpose of much of what Ezekiel said concerning Egypt and Tyre, during the siege of Jerusalem and just afterward, corresponded very closely to his other messages of judgment against Israel. They can be read as attacks on the false hopes of the exiles that something would surely happen to enable them to go back home soon. There is more to these texts than that, however, for we shall see that they also take up the question of the relationship of the Gentile nations to Yahweh. In the first group of oracles to be discussed the status of the nations is simply that of enemies of the chosen people, Israel, but in most of these passages it will be found that the nations have a relationship with Yahweh in their own right. To Christians, most of whom by ancestry and citizenship are members of the "Gentile nations," the theology of such passages is potentially very important, for it represents our direct and personal link with the OT, which is otherwise addressed to a people and a nation to which we do not belong.

Despite the natural relationship between Gentile Christians and the nations of the OT, which has just been suggested, the oracles against the nations have been very generally neglected in both preaching and scholarship. About one-tenth of the prophetic literature is devoted to the other nations, in oracles distributed among ten of the fifteen prophetic books. Later apocalyptic writers picked up elements of that material and included the names of some of the nations of the past as symbolic references to the impending universal judgment which they were predicting. Best known to us is the use of Babylon in the book of Revelation as a cipher or substitute name for Rome. In the more militant periods of Christian history the nations were identified with whoever happened to be one's enemy at the time, just as Christians identified themselves with Israel, and that made it possible to find very satisfying predictions of judgment upon those who were making life difficult. But very little other use has been made of these speeches on the nations, and in this era, when Christianity seems a bit more irenic than it has sometimes been in the past, most people have been at a loss to find anything useful in them. The quality of the oracles against the nations does vary considerably, but some of the most important for us are found in Ezekiel. Much that appears in them is of historical interest only, or can be taken as a contribution to the larger subject of the relationship to Yahweh of those who are not the chosen people, but there are also certain specific passages which have a peculiar relevance for our own time, when the power of the state has become so awesome. These are the texts which have been gathered below in the material titled *Hybris*.

Unfriendly Neighbors
(25:1—26:6; 28:20–26; 29:6b–9a)

At the beginning of this large section of Ezekiel's book there appears a series of short oracles against the neighbors of Judah, each of them having the same form and essentially the same content. There are two against the Ammonites (25:1–5, 6–7), followed by oracles against Moab, Edom, the Philistines, and Tyre. The form is the familiar prophetic pattern of *reason* and *announcement*; e.g., "*Because* you said, . . . , *therefore* I am handing you over . . ." (25:3–4). The content in each case condemns the nation for its treatment of Judah at the time of their great disaster. Now, when we read the rest of chapters 25—32 with care, we find another example of this combination of form and content, in one of the oracles against Egypt, 29:6b–9a. There is also one stray passage which it is tempting to include with these others, although the form is not identical. It is simply a word of judgment against Sidon (28:20–23), but if we guess that perhaps it might be a fragment, then we would have a hypothetical series of oracles against seven neighboring nations. That is a very interesting result, because long before this Amos had delivered a series of prophecies against seven neighbors of Israel, using this same form, and concluding with an oracle of judgment against Israel herself. Ezekiel might have followed that tradition, in the order: Ammon, Moab, Edom, Philistia, Tyre, Egypt, and Sidon (or Sidon and Egypt), and then, when additional materials concerning Tyre and Egypt were added the Egypt and Sidon oracles could have become dislocated from the original sequence. This hypothetical original order is mentioned only to point out a significant difference be-

tween these passages and the oracles in Amos, after which
these seem to have been patterned. Amos does not take a
nationalistic approach, condemning the nations for crimes
committed against Israel, but speaks instead of what we
might call crimes against humanity: atrocities in war (1:3,
11, 13; 2:1) and engaging in the slave trade (1:6, 9). Furthermore, his eighth oracle, concerning Israel, is also a word of
judgment so that as he has swept the horizon and then
turns to the center, thus all stands under the coming judgment of Yahweh. In contrast to this, Ezekiel uses the same
form and produces a similar series, but in each case (ex-
cluding Sidon, which has no reason-clause) condemns the
nation for a crime committed against Judah. Noting that
contrast, one is then tempted to pick up the one fragment in
these chapters which deals with the house of Israel, rather
than the foreign nations, 28:24–26, which directly follows
the Sidon text, and think of it as corresponding to Amos'
eighth oracle. If that is allowable, once again there is a significant contrast, for these verses are a promise of restoration, not a word of judgment.

These comparisons should help us to understand the significance of a group of passages which at first or second reading
may seem to be completely dispensible for the modern
reader. They presuppose the fall of Jerusalem and reflect
some knowledge of ways in which these peoples participated
in or reacted to that disaster. Most of them profited in some
way from it; in other cases they had an opportunity to help
Judean fugitives and refused to do it. And now another question of the justice of God has been raised for the survivors.
Does the house of Israel alone stand under judgment? Are the
Ammonites and the Philistines in any way responsible to
Yahweh, or does the fall of Jerusalem and the destruction of
Yahweh's temple leave them quite free to do as they please
without any fear of that formerly mighty God?

Here is another example of the "universalism" of the
prophets, that is, their insistence that all peoples have a relationship of some sort with Yahweh and that it is not Israel
alone that is responsible to him. The message of these oracles
is this: Jerusalem had to fall, but her neighbors were in no
way justified in taking advantage of that calamity for their
own enrichment and to increase the sufferings of those who

survived. These passages contain a message concerning the justice of God on an international scale, and they also served Ezekiel's audience as a preliminary to the promise of restoration. That was necessary, for the nations had left the exiles without a habitable place to which they could ever hope to return, and if a promise of return was to mean very much to them something would have to be done about those nations (28:24–26).

The Tragedy of Tyre (26:7—27:36)

Following the oracle against Tyre which condemns it for its reaction to the fall of Jerusalem (discussed in the preceding section, 26:1–6) comes a series of oracles using a variety of literary types. In 26:7–14 we find a detailed description, in advance of the desolation which will soon be brought upon Tyre by the armies of Nebuchadnezzar. This is followed by the depiction of a scene of lamentation over the death of Tyre (26:15–21) and by a lengthy allegory in which Tyre is depicted as a wealthy merchant ship which goes down at sea, followed once again by bitter lamentation (27:1–36). The reason for this extended treatment of a Phoenician city-state has been mentioned briefly earlier, but some additional comments need to be made to help explain the tone of these passages.

Until the attack by Nebuchadnezzar, Tyre had been a highly successful commercial city, the home of a fleet of merchant vessels which extended her trading empire to distant parts of the Mediterranean basin. The city-state had usually been on friendly terms with Israel and Judah. At the very beginning of the monarchy, King Hiram cooperated with David and Solomon, and the trading activities of the latter made use of Phoenician ships (1 Kings 9:26–28; 10:11–22). As merchants, the Phoenicians seem to have been more interested in preserving friendly relationships with potential customers than in the kind of squabbles over territory which characterized the other little kingdoms in the area. Tyre was a commercial rival of Jerusalem, then, but not a significant political threat, as far as we know, and they never seem to have been bitter enemies. It is a city denounced by Amos for engaging in the slave trade (1:9–10), but in the other prophetic books the dominant themes are the description of its wealth and overtones of lamentation (Isa 23; Zech 9:2-4; and Ezekiel).

Here is an aspect of the attitude of OT writers toward the world which is not always taken seriously by Christians. They are impressed by the wealth of Tyre and do not condemn it as such. Because of the Phoenician cruelty to slaves and their arrogant pride (to be discussed in the next section) Tyre does stand under the judgment of God, but the strong, prophetic reaction to that message is lamentation over the loss of the real material glories of that great city. These prophets did not fall prey to the temptation to gloat over another's misfortune, even when the other could be said to deserve it fully, even when the other was a more successful rival, as was certainly true of Tyre. Their enthusiastic descriptions of the wealth of Tyre, of which the allegory in Ezek 27 is the most impressive, and their laments over her fall represent an almost unnoticed but significant piece of evidence for the remarkable openness to the world which can be found in the prophetic books.

Hybris: When the State Becomes God
(28:1-19; 29:1-6a, 9b-12; 31:1-18; 32:1-16)

In these four remarkable passages Ezekiel produces a different kind of allegory. They have three things in common which set them off from the others in the book: The subjects are foreign kings, the imagery is borrowed from mythological material common to the ancient Near East, and the theme may be described most briefly by using a word borrowed from Greek, *hybris*. Why these allegories were written concerning the kings of Tyre and Egypt can best be explained by the importance of those two places in the minds of the exiles at that time; the reasons for the other two features will require a fairly lengthy explanation.

It is important to note that the subject in these passages is not the fall of Jerusalem, nor does it have anything explicit to do with the past, present, or future of Israel. The subject is kingship in two of Israel's influential neighbors, and since for the ancient world the king was the state, in theory if not in practice, we have in these texts a prophetic commentary on the nature of the state in the plan of Yahweh! These governments were far different from those of the late twentieth century, but as you read on you may find that there are some remarkable similarities as well.

Why the mythological stuff? Ezekiel's decision to draw his themes from those sources, when he began to talk about kingship, is highly significant. In 28:11–19 he takes the theme of the First Man in the Garden of God, known to us from Gen 2—3, but with parallels to be found in the mythology of the ancient Near East, and as he develops that in his own way, he emphasizes what? Perfection, wisdom, and beauty. Remember that he is talking about a pagan, a rival, the king of Tyre. We know little of the actual mythology of the Phoenicians in this period and less of their ideology of kingship, but do know that elsewhere the king could be assimilated to the First Man (the Adam) of the myths, as Ezekiel is doing here. As he did in the allegory of the ship so he does now in a far more extravagant and dangerous way— he emphasizes the real wealth, glory, and beauty of Tyre, now personified in its king.

So far the myth would take him. Nowhere else but in Genesis does the first created man sin and get expelled from the Garden as punishment, and nowhere in oriental kingship ideology is there anything to correspond to the condemnation of the king in 28:15b–16, 17b–18. Here the prophet becomes completely original, introducing iniquity, violence, pride, and unrighteousness into the Garden of God, and announcing that because of it the king of Tyre has or will come to a dreadful end. He cannot be judged against the standards of Sinai, as Israel is judged, but the prophet assumes there are certain standards which are applicable to all people, standards which Yahweh upholds.

The theology which lies behind this passage is made more explicit by the oracle which precedes it, in 28:1–10. In more straightforward language, without the use of allegory and introducing the traditional, prophetic "reason/announcement" form, Ezekiel addresses the king and states plainly the essence of the problem. His wisdom and wealth are not denied, but are reaffirmed. He is wiser than that legendary Daniel, the Syrian king known to us now from the Ugaritic texts found at Ras Shamra and mentioned also by Ezekiel in chapter 14. But he also claims to be as wise as a god, and more— he claims to be a god. This is where Yahweh draws the line.

Wisdom and beauty and wealth are by no means to be condemned in themselves, for they are the creations and the gifts of God. But when a human being is not willing to be satisfied with all that and wants to take that last step, to be one's own god, that is what the Greeks called *hybris*, self-deifying pride, and at that point Yahweh must intrude with a blunt reminder of who is God after all.

But can any human being really make any claim to divinity significant enough for Yahweh to bother himself with? Ordinarily the OT considers pride of that kind to be rather laughable and the source of its own destruction, but there is one case where it takes such claims seriously. When it is a king who claims to be a god, that is, when the state makes such a claim, that is seen by the prophets to be different from individual pride, for the state really can become a virtual god to its subjects. This is why Ezekiel chooses material from mythology, which originally dealt with the realm of the divine, and why he dared to speak of foreign kings in those terms. His allegories exalt the king (the state) nearly to the rank of deity in order to express the truth about their real power and glory. The state does assume the right to determine what is right and wrong for its citizens and claims the power of life and death over them. With the power and wealth which the state can accumulate it can accomplish marvelous works which are impossible for any individual to undertake. None of these things is considered to be wrong; these achievements of the great states are a cause for wonder rather than condemnation. It is only when the state refuses to acknowledge that there may be any power greater than it, anything to which the state itself may be held responsible, that is, when it begins to deify itself, that it becomes a devil and not a god, and the one God, Yahweh, must intervene. The problem is that no human being, no state is wise enough or good enough to be a god, and when the rights of God himself begin to be arrogated by some institution with the power enough to try to behave like a god, it is bestiality, rather than divinity, which results. Fortunately for humanity there is one absolute difference between Yahweh and everything else that lives, and that is mortality. "Will you still say, 'I am a god,' in the presence of those who slay you?" Kings die and states die, and as we think about the history of tyranny we may find that can be affirmed as a great blessing.

Some of what has been said in the preceding paragraphs already presupposes and comments on the other *hybris*-texts in this section, so before more is said the details of those passages should be discussed.

In 29:1–6a and 32:1–8 the prophet identifies the king of Egypt with some great aquatic monster, the *tannim* in Hebrew, translated "dragon" in the RSV. Since its home is the Nile, this may be a mythologized form of the crocodile (so interpreted by TEV), which was worshiped as a deity in Egypt. There were monsters of various kinds in the myths of the ancient Near East, some of them beneficent, some of them dangerous, but the most frequent theme involving such beings was that of conflict between a hero (usually a god) and the monster, leading to the destruction of the latter. Ezekiel has been influenced by that theme, for he does not find it possible to use the dragon to depict the glories of kingship, as he does the First Man and Cosmic Tree symbols, and the main emphasis is on combat and destruction. He does find a way to bring in *hybris*, in 29:3, however, when he quotes the Pharaoh as saying, "My Nile is my own; I made myself" (as in the Hebrew; most modern translations prefer to follow the versions, which read, "I made it."). There is an Egyptian hymn which speaks of the Nile as producing itself, and in royal texts the king is praised as having the Nile under his control, suggesting that Ezekiel may have had some accurate knowledge of Egyptian lore. Of course, the Pharaoh was explicitly deified in Egyptian religion and the prophet may very well have been aware of that. At any rate, the one condemnation of the Egyptian king which he sees fit to introduce is that claim to creative power. Associated with the mythological material in chapter 29, as in 28, is a reason/announcement oracle, in vss. 9b–12, and once again the charge has nothing to do with Israel, but only with the self-exaltation of that foreign king.

In chapter 31 the theme of the Cosmic Tree is developed at considerable length. In mythology the Cosmic or World Tree represented the entire created world. Its branches symbolized the heavens, its roots extended down to the netherworld, and around its trunk lived all the creatures of the earth. It was an entirely positive symbol, and Ezekiel describes it with considerable enthusiasm, it seems in vss. 3–9. What is astonishing, for a prophet of Israel, is that he compares the Pharaoh in all his glory with that cosmic symbol. Once again there is a strong measure of acceptance of the earthly glories of a great kingdom; the value of its accomplishments is not to be denied. But there is a point beyond which the state may not go without bringing great harm into the world, and that is the attitude described earlier. "Because it towered high and set its top among the clouds, and its heart was proud of its height, I will give it into the hand of a mighty one of the nations; he shall surely deal with it as its wickedness deserves" (vss. 10–11). Ezekiel shatters the honored myth of the Cosmic Tree by announcing that its personification, the Pharaoh, is going to be cut down. The prophetic word, in the form of a reason and an announcement, has just been quoted, but in this case Ezekiel seems to find more potential for allegorizing in this material and he expands the word of judgment with a description of the fall of the great tree. The allegory becomes a bit hard to follow near the end when he has the tree go down to Sheol to join the trees of Eden, but the reason for introducing Sheol is not so hard to understand. It is because death is understood by the prophet to be God's last word to those who claim to be gods.

With the enormous power which governments can wield over their people it has been tempting for them to claim virtual divinity for themselves, and some have found it impossible to resist the temptation. In our century the classical example seems still to be the Third Reich, which developed an entire mythology to support its claims and which attempted to sustain what Toynbee called "the illusion of immortality," with its slogan, the Thousand Year Reich. But even Hitler's methods of attempting to exercise absolute power over his subjects have already begun to seem rather primitive, compared to those which are available today. Frederick the Great's saying, "My people and I have come to an arrangement which satisfies us both. They are to say what they please, and I am to do what I please," represents a far more liberal attitude than the modern state finds it necessary to accept. But it did not take the experience of the Third Reich to reveal the truth that the state which attempts to become a god to its people, accepting no responsibility to any power higher than itself, will become instead a monster, the source of destruction and degradation. Long ago, Ezekiel already began to understand that and he transformed the propaganda of his time—those myths—with a prophetic word which put things in their proper order. We need to do some translating and interpreting of his words for our time, but there surely can be no question about their relevance.

Egypt Also Has a Future (29:13–16)

Another of the remarkable contributions of Ezekiel to OT theology appears in this short and little-noticed passage. It is another example of how the prophets began to find a place for the other nations in a world governed by only one God, the God of Israel. The preceding unit, vss. 9b–12, predicts a sweeping judgment of Egypt because of the *hybris* of her king, a judgment which involves making the country an utter waste and desolation for forty years. But added to that threat is this passage, predicting restoration. It is clear what has happened. As the prophet considered Egypt's future, he thought that Yahweh would deal with Egypt as he dealt with Israel, and so he speaks of an exile for a fixed period of years, followed by a return to their own land. Egypt had been such a perennial threat to Israel that he must add the assurance that in the future they will be a lowly kingdom, no longer able to cause trouble for anyone, but the very fact that he thinks of an independent future at all for the old enemy, and finds it appropriate to apply the same pattern to Israel and to Egypt is a remarkable development. That idea is taken even further in a part of Isaiah which is probably later than the book of Ezekiel, Isa 19:18–25, the high point of universalism in the OT.

When Prophecy Failed (29:17–20)

This is a passage of considerable interest and importance for our understanding of OT prophecy, but since it is not likely to be a text which is very useful for preaching purposes, it cannot be discussed here as fully as it might be. It is dated much later than the other oracles concerning the nations, in 571 B.C., and it refers directly back to what Ezekiel had predicted in 586 concerning Nebuchadnezzar's total destruction of Tyre. That never happened. After thirteen years under siege the city finally came to terms. It was not destroyed and Nebuchadnezzar gained very little booty from it, for the same ships which had been bringing in supplies for all those years had been used to remove all the valuables before they surrendered. The news of the debacle had reached Babylonia and Ezekiel has a comment to make about it. Notice that he does not find it necessary to defend or explain away his earlier prophecy; in effect he just admits that it didn't happen. The failure of a prediction to come true in every detail thus does not appear to have been considered any great scandal. They must have understood prophecy in a way different from those who believe it must involve one hundred percent accurate predictions. Ezekiel acknowledges that it didn't happen as he had said it would and then offers a new prediction, that Egypt will be given to Nebuchadnezzar. What makes the passage doubly interesting is that this prediction did not come true, either. Nebuchadnezzar did invade Egypt shortly thereafter, but was unsuccessful. Neither failure led the believing community in exile to dismiss Ezekiel as a false prophet, however. They must have recognized, as we can, with the advantage of the perspective of history, that this man did understand the essential truth about what God was doing in the world, and it was that, rather than the ability to predict the accurate details of coming events, which made him a true prophet.

The Day of the Lord (30:1–26)

This chapter is a lengthy description of the Day of Yahweh in very traditional language. Echoes of Amos and especially of the first chapter of Zephaniah are evident, and with the exception of a few distinctive elements the chapter could have been written by almost any prophet. It is a significant passage for those who want to study the development of the concept of the Day of Yahweh, but since it lacks the theological creativity which has been characteristic of most of the other oracles against the nations, it seems appropriate not to devote much attention to it here.

Sheol (32:17–32)

The place of the dead, Sheol or the Pit, is seldom described in the OT. There are passing references to it here and there, such as in Job and the Psalms, but the most extensive comments on it occur in Ezek 26—32 and in Isa 14:4–21, all of which deal with foreigners! The OT is reticent about saying very much at all concerning the state of the dead, probably because the Israelites had found the Canaanite cult of the dead to be overly enticing, and the fact that foreign kings are dealt with in these texts may explain why the authors were willing to speak more freely. In addition to these verses in chapter 32 you may also consult 26:19–21 and 31:15–18. Ordinarily it is doubtful that these texts would be preached as they are, but they clearly can be useful as background for the preparation of sermons, based on other texts, which deal with the biblical understanding of death.

One comment about the development of that understanding will be offered in connection with this text. Sheol is just a kind of community grave, where everyone goes when they die. It is not a place of bliss or of punishment, as OT writers understand it. Eventually, new ideas in abundance will be associated with the place of the dead, as we well know, and it may be that the very beginnings of one of them may be found in Ezek 32. It seems to be a special disgrace for the king of Egypt to have to lie down with the uncircumcised and those slain by the sword. Recent studies have shown that the first of those terms referred to infants who died before they could be circumcised and thus had not formally become members of the covenant people, and probably were not buried in the family tomb. "Those slain by the sword" indicates people who have been murdered or killed in battle and never properly buried. Popular belief was that both of these fates left the dead person in an unfortunate condition of some sort, but now a prophet declares that for *moral reasons* the king of Egypt will share that same misery. This doesn't go very far toward a teaching about punishment for one's sins after death, but it does seem to be an early step in that direction.

Edom (35:1–15)

In addition to the brief oracle against Edom which is a part of the series in chapter 25, three short oracles appear in the midst of the promises of restoration for the exiles, apparently interrupting the depiction of a peaceful future with more threats of judgment. Some reasons for its location can be ascertained, however. Chapter 36 begins with a reference to claims which an enemy has made against the mountains of Israel, and the historical fact is that after the Babylonian successes in Palestine, the Edomites began to move westward across the Arabah into the southern regions of old Judah. Ezekiel's promises of restoration thus were challenged by the occupation of parts of the land by other people, and so he deals here with Edom as a special problem (note vs. 10 and compare it with 36:2). Although that problem is very much a thing of the past for us, the role played by the Edomites in the Bible is intriguing enough that a brief comment on it may be found useful in preaching from other texts in which Esau, Edom, or the Idumaeans appear.

Israel recognized its close relationship with the Edomites by tracing their genealogy back to Esau, brother of their own ancestor, Jacob. No negative comment is ever made about their religion, which has led to the suggestion that it may have been similar to Yahwism, but they were relatives who often did not get along well. The Edomites suffered under David, and they made the Judeans suffer at the time of the fall of Jerusalem, refusing them sanctuary and selling them into slavery instead. For their treatment of refugees at that time and for their later infiltration into Judean territory they earned the continuing bitter hatred of the Jews (reflected in Obadiah and elsewhere). But in NT times their descendants still occupied the region, Idumaea, derived from the old name Edom. The Idumaeans were forcibly converted to Judaism when the region was conquered by the Jewish Hasmonean family in the second century B.C. and they appear one more time in Jewish history with a vengeance when Herod the Great was made king of Palestine by the Romans. For Herod was an Idumaean, Jewish by faith due to that earlier conversion but a descendant of the hated Edomites.

Reprise and Turning Point
(Ezekiel 33:21–33)

Chapter 33 represents the turning point of the book of
Ezekiel, for in its midst is recorded the arrival of a fugitive
who brings the news that Jerusalem has fallen. It is distinctly
set off from the oracles against the nations which precede it
and from the allegory of the sheep and their shepherds which
follows. This makes it important to try to understand why
the five separate units contained in the chapter have been
grouped together as they have.

Jerusalem Has Fallen (33:21–22)

The first two passages are alternate forms of texts which
have already appeared earlier in the book. The description of
Ezekiel's call to be a watchman is also found in 3:16–21, and
the defense of Yahweh's justice is a shorter form of the material in chapter 18. In our consideration of 3:16–21 it was
noted that many scholars believe the designation of Ezekiel
as a watchman, responsible for the lives of individuals, more
properly belongs at this point in his career, when in reality
there was no more Israel, but only individual survivors to
whom he could minister. It was suggested there that this re-
definition of his work, which chronologically belongs in
chapter 33, was also inserted in chapter 3 as a supplement to
this original call when the book was put into its present
form, so as to present a more complete picture of his work at
the beginning of the book. It is less obvious whether his ap-
peals to individuals to repent (vss. 10–20) also first became a
part of his work at this time, or whether they formed a part
of his message before 587, as the location of chapter 18
suggests.

At any rate, both passages are appropriately located here,
in conjunction with the message that Jerusalem had fallen.
That terrible event validated the truth of the prophet's earlier messages, but it should be noted that he makes no mention of that. The simple report of the fact will suffice, but its
implications hang heavily over the survivors, even though

they are left unspoken. This is why the report is preceded by accounts of Ezekiel's commission to work with individuals, calling them to repentance. They contain an assurance that a future is still possible for them and make it clear what human beings can still do in order to have a chance.

These two hopeful passages which precede the report of Jerusalem's fall are balanced by two reminders that a complacent assumption that things are bound to get better now is totally without foundation.

A Futile Grasp for Hope (33:23-29)

After the Babylonians secured control of Judah they attempted to reestablish a local government under the leadership of Gedaliah, as 2 Kings 25:22-26 and Jer 40—41 record, but Gedaliah was soon murdered and it is likely that life for those left in Palestine remained rather chaotic for some time, although there is little available information about those years. One fragment appears in these verses: a report concerning the attitude of some of those left in the land after 587. Here is another of those quotations to which Ezekiel responds: "Abraham was only one man, yet he got possession of the land; but we are many; the land is surely given us to possess." We learn from this that the attitude of superiority toward those who had been exiled or had fled the land, to which Ezekiel referred earlier (11:15), still existed after the fall of Jerusalem. How much information the prophet in exile had about those people and their situation we do not know, but his description of them is what we might suspect of the aftermath of a war which had left Judah desolate and the remaining people without leadership. He speaks of idolatry and murder and adultery as characteristic of the lives of those very people who once again are affirming their "faith" that the promise of the land to Abraham must surely also be valid for them. The prophet's response is the old, familiar threat: sword, wild beasts, and pestilence. At this point it is clearly a message for the exiles themselves, who were still in shock from learning that their hopes for return to Jerusalem were totally in vain, and who must have felt completely alone and cut off from all the old promises, not least because of the news of this superior attitude of those who still remained in the land. Part of Ezekiel's work of reconstruction

thus had to include the insistence that there was no future in
the land, the future was to begin with the exiles.

The Preacher's Lament (33:30–33)

Once more we hear what the exiles have been saying, and
this time (as in 20:49) it is a saying about the prophet himself. We discover that he has achieved a certain measure of
popularity. They come to hear him regularly, for he tells such
fascinating stories and his words entrance them with their
power, but he is little more than an entertainer. The title,
"Preacher's Lament" has been chosen for this section because it speaks of something which surely every preacher
knows very well: "They come to you as people come, and
they sit before you as my people, and they hear what you say
but they will not do it." If this passage is located in the correct place, chronologically, then what it says is that so far
Ezekiel has accomplished virtually nothing. Perhaps the
early antagonism to him has died down, but he is not making
converts. The work of creating a new and faithful community
in exile still lies ahead of him, and he tells the exiles plainly
how futile he understands his speaking and their listening to
have been so far, in one more attempt to break through their
defenses.

To try to preach on this whole chapter might be something
of a *tour de force*, but one might consider what the various
parts, taken together, say about Starting Over. There is the
receipt of bitter news (vss. 21–22) accompanied by a typical
human response, the effort to deny that one door in life has
been permanently closed (vss. 23–29). In the effort to counter
hopelessness there is the assurance that the future is still
open to those who are willing to make a change for the better
(vss. 1–20), but that is paired with the warning that just listening to comforting words without doing anything about
them is a course of ultimate futility (vss. 30–33).

Sheep and Their Shepherds
(Ezekiel 34:1-31)

Preaching the Promises of Ezekiel

The restoration promises in this book seem to be far easier to preach than words of judgment, but some general comments on the appropriate use of them are called for before we consider them in detail. Because they were addressed to exiles, the promise which is repeated most often is that of return to the land. That does not appear to be a subject which is of direct relevance to Christians at all, for the NT did not appropriate the promise of residence in the land of Canaan and say it applies to all Christians. It is true that some have attempted to combine all the eschatological material in the Bible into one, comprehensive, final drama, and have thus found a place for the future return of the Jews to the Promised Land as one stage, one sign that the end is near, but that involves a good many dubious exegetical procedures. Other Christians have usually just ignored the promises of return to the land. Our tradition has focused instead on any passage which could be called "messianic," that is a prediction of the coming of Jesus. That would point immediately to the references to David in chapters 34 and 37, but it must be noted that the figure of David plays a rather minor role in Ezekiel's eschatology. The promise of the new heart and new spirit in chapter 36 has a clear and direct relationship to the NT, but other assurances, such as the complete absence of hunger in the future (34:29), have quite obviously not come true yet. Hence we are confronted in these futuristic passages by emphases which are different from our own, by some promises which seem to have come true, by some which certainly have not, and by some which do not even interest us.

A full discussion of the various ways in which Christian theology has dealt with the promises of the OT is not possible here, but one approach will be suggested which will provide the background for the comments which will be made on the individual chapters. Christians have tended to deny any significant fulfillment of these texts in the history of Judaism between the time of Ezekiel and that of Christ, because of their desire to affirm that Christ is the complete fulfillment of all God's promises. But there are two problems with this. The first is that we Christians also have an eschatology, so admittedly we still wait for the fulfillment of much that is promised in both Testaments. The second is that an unbiased reading of Jewish history strongly suggests that Jews also have been the beneficiaries of partial fulfillments. For example, some Jews did return to the Promised Land and the temple was rebuilt. Restoration did occur in part in the years following Ezekiel's ministry.

The approach to be taken here affirms that all of Jewish and Christian experience involves hope for that which God is yet to do, and all of it involves the experience of fulfillments of that hope—but until the eschaton comes they are *all* partial fulfillments. This allows Christians to accept with enthusiasm the evidence of God's saving work with the Jewish people in the post-exilic period without compromising their belief in the uniqueness of Christ, for even though we affirm our belief that all God's promises are fulfilled in him, the fact is that we do not experience them all in their fullness as yet, and will not until the end comes. Both Testaments, then are books of promise and fulfillment, testimonies both to the experience of God's saving work and to hope for the completion of his salvation.

From Judgment to Blessing

One of the new elements in Ezekiel's work is the comprehensive picture of successive periods in Israel's history of promise, rebellion, judgment, and restoration. Certainly all those elements are to be found in the books of earlier prophets, but they occur in separate pericopes, so that we cannot be sure that any one before Ezekiel projected in advance that precise course of events. Amos spoke of exile as the end, for example, without any indication of life for Israel beyond that, and the two promise oracles at the conclusion of the book are not unified with the rest of his message. Because of this, many doubt that the promises come from Amos and date them at a later period, but even if they are his, there is nothing in his work to show how he would make the theological move from judgment to restoration. The same is true for the other pre-exilic prophets, although Hosea does make some effort in that direction in his reversal of salvation history, in chapter 2. It is very likely that Jeremiah did make the transition from words of judgment to promises of restoration within his own career, as Ezekiel did, but he does not put the whole story together in so thoroughgoing a way. What is so important about Ezekiel's contribution is that he is careful to show *how* it is possible that a new and blessed future can be created from the pitiful remains of the house of Israel. One example of the move from the history of rebellion to God's transformed future has already appeared in chapter 20; now two more comprehensive pictures of judgment and salvation appear in chapters 34 and 36.

The Imagery of Sheep and Shepherds (34:1–10)

No explanation of the allegory in this chapter was required by Ezekiel's audience, for the imagery was well-known to everyone in his day, but the modern reader requires a little help. One of the common titles for kings in the ancient Near East was "shepherd," for the ideology of kingship included the belief that the ruler was to feed and protect his people. When Ezekiel spoke of the "shepherds of Israel," then, those who heard him would immediately think of the ruling families of Judah, or of that series of inept kings who had succeeded Josiah. Jeremiah had pronounced judgment on those same kings and his sequence of oracles in chapter 22 is concluded by an oracle against "the shepherds who destroy and scatter the sheep," in 23:1–4. Ezekiel begins this chapter as if it were more of his condemnations of the sins of Judah before 587, but the passage is not out of place, for this is his way of moving from the time of judgment to the coming blessings. We see in vss. 5–6 that the judgment has already come, so that the words against the shepherds are leading, via the condemnation of those rulers, directly to promises for the sheep. (Note the similar words in Matt 9:36.) These initial verses thus describe one aspect of Israel's past life which God will have to change before the better future can be expected. Note that there is no appeal to the shepherds to change, for it is too late for that. Neither are these verses simply a justification of the judgment which has befallen them. Instead they establish the contrast between the past and the future; between their shepherding and God's. The main subject is really the sheep and their fate, for they have a future with a different sort of shepherd.

Movement Toward a Different Future (34:11–16)

God is the sole source and agent of salvation. Note that there is no reference to human activity of any kind in this chapter except for the contrasting work of the worthless shepherds and the new David. Although Ezekiel speaks of repentance and of internal change elsewhere, that is omitted here, for the entire emphasis is on the saving activity of God. "Behold, I, I myself will search for my sheep." Notice also that the promises are concerned only with material benefits, in contrast with chapter 36 and others.

The activities of the worthless shepherds have resulted in exile for God's people (vs. 6) and hence the first promise is that of gathering the dispersed people and returning them to the Promised land (vss. 11–13). The prophet does not insist on preserving his allegory intact, when it is not convenient to do so, and so we find realistic language appearing in vs. 13, for it would make no sense to think of sheep being gathered from other peoples and countries. But the allegory resumes as he describes the life of the sheep in their own country, with a new shepherd, God himself. This also is not new imagery, for God was affirmed to be king over Israel, and thus the concept of the king as shepherd was also applied to Yahweh (see Ps 23). The benefits which are described at first are return, healing, and feeding, all of which can be transferred from sheep to people without much need for interpretation.

God Sorts His Flock (34:17–22)

In chapter 20 Ezekiel introduced a time of purging in the wilderness, by which God was expected to prepare those who were returning from exile in order that only those who were ready to participate in the life of the new people of God would be permitted to enter the Promised Land. In that passage it was idolatry which particularly concerned the prophet. He knew better than to think that everyone who passed through the experience of exile would automatically qualify to become a member of the faithful people which God was at work to create. So in this chapter also he introduces an episode of judgment in which God sorts out those who have disrupted the peace of the community. It is an ethical issue rather than a cultic one which Ezekiel recognizes in this case. Note that even though no human activity is overtly referred to as a basis for salvation, some responsibility for one's own future is certainly implied in these verses. There is an echo of this passage in Matt 25:32.

The Covenant of Peace (34:23–31)

We see that the Promised Land was believed to be so central to the covenant relationship between Yahweh and Israel that whenever a new future for the people of God is envisioned it begins with the promise of restoration to that place. In addition God here promises that they will have a new earthly king, who is simply called David. God is to be their shepherd, he has promised in vs. 15, but he always works through human beings in this life, and so David is also called their shepherd. Is this a resurrection of the original, tenth-century king of Israel? It seems very unlikely that Ezekiel or his contemporaries would have thought of such a thing, for the expectation of resurrection was not commonplace in Israel at this time. (More on this in connection with chap. 37.) It will be one of the "Davids," that is, a member of the house of David, who will become the future, righteous king. Note that he is not expected to function as a savior in any sense; he will feed his flock and be their shepherd, which simply means that he will do what the kingship ideology had always declared the king was supposed to do. To convert this into modern terminology, strange as it may seem at first, this is a promise that God's people will enjoy good government after they are purged of those who are destructive of the peace and restored to their own land. We can call this David a messianic figure, for the word "messiah" is used of royal figures in most of its OT passages, but this is not the promise Jesus fulfilled. To be exact it is the one he refused to fulfill, understanding that earthly kingship was not his mission (see John 6:15). Jesus does clearly allude to Ezek 34 in his discourse on the good shepherd and his sheep in John 10:1–18, but he does some original things with it. The contrast between the true shepherd and his worthless predecessors is still present, but when Jesus declares himself to be the good shepherd (vs. 11) he makes it immediately clear that this is no claim to kingship. "The good shepherd lays down his life for his sheep." That is not in the OT tradition and represents something new in the NT message of salvation.

Ezekiel does not use the term "new covenant," which occurs only one place in the OT (Jer 31:31–34), but he does think of a different covenant, which he calls the covenant of peace in vs. 25 and in 37:26. The covenant of peace focuses on material blessings, especially security and an abundance of food. Whether the wild beasts of vs. 25 are real wild animals (realistic language, as in 2 Kings 17:25 and Ezek 14:15) or are allegorical representations of the enemy nations remains uncertain, since we have seen that the prophet can shift back and forth from allegory to literal speech. But in vss. 27b–28a there is no question that the kind of security which is promised is physical peace in this world.

Christian eschatology has tended many times to be so spiritual and otherworldly that the promises of this chapter may seem to some to be rather shortsighted. They do not speak of forgiveness of sins or eternal life, but of living safely in a fertile land under a just government. For some Christians that doesn't even have anything to do with "religion"! Here, then, is where the OT challenges us to take another look at what we have been taught, if ours is a faith which concerns itself only with the "spiritual," for this first part of the canon knows nothing of a God who does not intend to bless the whole person he has made, rather than just saving their souls. At its best, Christianity has always understood that, but the temptation to despise this world and these bodies which God has given us in favor of some better world hereafter has also always been present. Is the OT wrong in putting such an emphasis on material things, or is it also the Word of God to us, attempting to correct the persistent error? That is an important issue for every Christian's theology, and it should be addressed in preaching from time to time, since there is so much confusion about it.

Salvation includes not only human beings and human society but also the world of nature, as these verses show, and Ezekiel will provide more evidence for that in chapters 36 and 47. The full range of transformations which Israel anticipated in God's future will be discussed in more detail in the next section. If we ask, Is there nothing in this chapter which was fulfilled by Jesus in his first advent? the answer is, Of course there is. The chapter concludes with God's promise: "And they shall know that I, the Lord their God, am with them, and that they, the house of Israel are my people." Here is another reference to the covenant, in the formula, "they are my people," but the promise, "I am with them" is taken up explicitly in the NT with the affirmation that in Jesus that came true. Matthew quotes Isa 7:14, with its name Immanuel and translates the Hebrew name into Greek so that his readers cannot fail to understand what the birth of Jesus means: God is with us. John also speaks of Jesus' birth in the same way, "And the Word became flesh and dwelt among us" (John 1:14). Israel's hope for the time to come when God would truly dwell in their midst did come true in the Incarnation, Christians believe. As for the other promises of this chapter, the return of the Diaspora to the Promised Land did begin in 538 B.C. and that restoration should not be downgraded as a thing of no importance in the plan of God, even though it was not accompanied by the establishment of a new Davidic king or the gifts of security and abundant fertility. We still await the coming of those gifts, but if Christians believe that in the church the Spirit of Christ is already at work to bring us a foretaste of the eschaton, then perhaps passages such as these should serve as a challenge to us to do what we can now, so that already now people can find a measure of security and freedom from want through the church. We can at least be the sign to them that those promises are true and that they are already coming true.

Israel's New Life
(Ezekiel 36:1–38)

The first part of this chapter (vss. 1–15) shows a close relationship with chapter 35. Both passages are addressed toward mountains, the former toward the mountains of Edom and the latter toward the mountains of Israel, and when read together they present a striking, double contrast. At present Edom has a bright future ahead of it, with the desolate hills of Judah lying ready for occupation. But the future will be utterly different from what they think. The day is coming when the mountains of Edom will be desolate and the mountains of Judah, now bereft of everything, will once again flourish and become a home for the house of Israel. In the division of the book, we might thus have taken 35:1—36:15 as a unit, but for our purposes it seemed better to take Edom along with the other oracles against the nations, and to think of chapter 36 as another of Ezekiel's efforts to display the transition from judgment to blessing.

No More Reproach for the Mountains of Israel
(36:1–15)

As chapter 34 began with reference to the sufferings of the people under unworthy shepherds, so chapter 36 begins by speaking of the way the land has suffered under the depredations of the nations. As God punished the shepherds for their mistreatment of the sheep, so also now God intends to turn the reproach which the mountains of Israel have suffered back on the nations which are responsible for it. Once again, a text which sounds partly like a judgment passage is actually transitional, speaking of the wrongs which God now must correct in order for blessing to come.

Since the land of Canaan itself was a central part of the covenant relationship between God and Israel, then it is not surprising that Ezekiel should address the land, as if it could hear him, in order to justify his promises of new life for his people. The question which had tormented the exiles ever since 597 was this: How can a people exist and maintain their identity without a land they can call their own? That remains a highly significant question to our own day, for in this century of the displaced person there are groups such as Armenians, Lithuanians, and Vietnamese who are trying to do that very thing. The continuing existence of the Jews as a diaspora people for many centuries shows it can be done, and yet it is that same group which continues to insist that it must have a land. There is a certain paradox, a tension and a danger, in being a people without a land. So we have seen that in every promise so far, restoration to the land and the restoration of the land play an important role.

What the exiles may have known about the situation in Canaan after 587 would have made their hopes for return seem even more futile. In this chapter Ezekiel alludes to the glee with which the neighboring nations speak of the desolation of Judah, for it left something of a vacuum of which they fully intended to take advantage. We have already noted briefly the gradual migration of the Edomites into what had been southern Judah, and the books of Ezra and Nehemiah reveal that Ammonites and Philistines and the rulers of Samaria continued to attempt to wield political power in Judah not only before the return of exiles began but for long after. God's promise to free the hills of their land from the threats of the neighboring nations was thus addressed to a very real and practical problem.

The Divine Motive (36:16–23)

As in 20:42–44, Ezekiel now describes with care, but very bluntly, the real reason why any Jew can expect to return to the Promised Land, or even to hope to have a relationship with Yahweh anywhere. Christians call it being saved by grace alone, but the prophet uses a different vocabulary. It is for the sake of Yahweh's holy name that they will be given a new future.

The continuity between this paragraph and the preceding one is to be found in the prophet's description of the defiling of that land, not by the nations but by its own inhabitants. The nations now play a different role, that of spectators (as in chap. 5) who ought to be brought to some measure of knowledge of God by what they see in Israel, but who have instead been led to scorn for Israel and her God (vs. 20), because of Israel's behavior and the punishment they have justly suffered for it. God's purpose, which we see to be broader than the salvation of Israel alone, has thus been temporarily thwarted, and the issue for Ezekiel is whether it is possible for the intention of God to be defeated by human resistance.

The key term for this prophet is God's "holy name," his way of referring to the essential nature of God himself. He must be faithful to that, the prophet announces. Even though there is nothing worth saving in Israel, no basis for reform, God has a purpose which he has committed to Israel, and that purpose will be carried out in spite of every obstacle. Ezekiel does not speak of the love of God, as other prophets do, and as the NT does, and his theology seems deficient for that reason. Perhaps he does not use it because love suggests there is something love*able* in the object of one's attentions, and Ezekiel emphasizes that is in no way true of Israel. It is God's continuing willingness to work with the unlovable, simply because he is God, which Ezekiel celebrates. That may have a negative ring to it, since it obviously has nothing good whatever to say about human beings. The concept of "total depravity" has not been a popular one at all in modern theology and especially in popular religion, despite the abundance of examples pointing to its truth in the history of this century. But there is a very important positive side to what Ezekiel says. There very probably were others in exile who came to conclusions about the *human* possibility of creating a new future which were just as pessimistic as Ezekiel's. To those people, what Ezekiel says in these verses, "And I will vindicate the holiness of my great name, . . . when through you I vindicate my holiness before their eyes," would come as great good news.

For those who have not been deceived by the optimism of humanistic dreams and recognize how thoroughly our societies and our selves have been permeated by evil, the message that there is a God who intends to do good for us, who has the power to do good no matter how much evil we produce, and who has the will to accomplish his purpose no matter how many obstacles we put in his way, is gospel indeed.

The Three-Fold Promise (36:24–38)

Ezekiel's most comprehensive picture of the future which God intends to create appears in this chapter, and it may be taken as an outline by which all of OT eschatology can be organized. He speaks of the transformation of human society, the transformation of the human person, and the transformation of nature. The OT does not express a hope for salvation *from* this world, but for the salvation *of* this world. Israelites did not look for freedom from the human body but for the perfection of the human body. They took creation theology seriously and believed that God made a world which was intended to be very good. Their eschatology acknowledged that sin had quite thoroughly corrupted everything, including the world of nature, but hope affirmed that God has a Day when he will transform it all in order to make everything right. Ezekiel does not include every aspect of Israel's hope in these verses (the most important omission is the glorification of Zion), but they do contain one of the Bible's most helpful outlines of the hope of Israel.

The Transformation of Human Society

This is the theme which most frequently appears in the futuristic texts of the OT, revealing that the corporate sense characteristic of old Israel was still very strong in the exilic and post-exilic periods. As usual, the promise begins with the return from exile (vs. 24), for the OT speaks of the blessed future as a time when people will live undisturbed in their own land (vs. 28). The city, which strikes some of us as a mixed blessing, will not be done away with in favor of some purely pastoral existence. Cities will be inhabited and waste places rebuilt (vss. 33, 37–38). It was more obvious then, perhaps, than it is now (when virtually all of life has been urbanized, no matter where we happen to reside), that it is the city which makes civilization possible, and that is to be affirmed and purified, not denied. Future relationships among the nations of the world, which play an important role in other eschatological texts, are only alluded to briefly here, expressing that concern for them to come to a knowledge of Yahweh (vs. 36). The king, representing government and the internal stability of Israelite society, is not mentioned at all in this chapter, but we did find that concern expressed in 34:23.

The Transformation of the Human Person

This is the special emphasis of chapter 36. Ezekiel has been so thoroughly convinced that Israel is "a nation of rebels" (2:3) that he sees no hope for the future except in God alone, as we have seen earlier. The prophet understands that merely returning to the Promised Land and rebuilding its cities will not solve the essential problem, which is human nature, and so he now promises radical changes in people themselves. First they must be cleansed, forgiven; the evil effects of all that they had done in the past must somehow be eradicated. Only God can do anything about the past, but Ezekiel promises that God intends to do just that (vss. 25, 29a, 33a). Even that miracle is not enough, however, for if we have a chance to make a fresh start and go at it with the same old equipment, the results are likely to be just as bad as before. A truly radical change must occur; the re-creation of the human person. "A new heart I will give you, and a new spirit I will put within you." In Hebrew anthropology the heart was not so much the seat of the emotions, as it is for us, as the location of the rational will. One thinks with the heart, in the OT, and makes decisions with the heart (see Isa 10:7; Ps 140;1–2; Ezek 3:7). The spirit is what animates the body, in some texts (as we shall see in Ezek 37), and is the source of power which makes possible special feats, elsewhere. When heart and spirit are brought together as they are here it has been said that if the heart represents the will, then the spirit represents the power to carry out the decisions of the will. What Ezekiel promises, then, is a re-creation of human beings which will make obedience possible (vs. 27). He does not think that God somehow did it wrongly at the beginning, for the transformation involves giving people hearts of *flesh*. There is nothing wrong with flesh, in the OT, for that is the way God made us. What is wrong is that our hearts of flesh, which had the potential for deciding to obey God, have become so calloused by continual disobedience that they have become virtually petrified, and we are trapped in our commitment to rebellion until God intervenes.

The closest parallel to this text in the OT is Jer 31:31–34, the promise of the new covenant. Ezekiel does not speak of covenant at all in this chapter, but Jeremiah's promise that God will put his law within them and write it upon their hearts, so that all will know him, shows that each prophet had the same kind of transformation in mind. These two texts are, of course, of great importance for the NT. Paul alludes to Ezek 36 in 1 Thess 4:1–12 and in 2 Cor 3:1–11, while Jeremiah's new covenant is alluded to in 1 Cor 11:25; Gal 4:21–28; and 1 John 2:7–8, and the passage itself is quoted in Heb 8:6–13 and 10:14–18. The affirmation that the radical, internal change promised by the OT has come to pass in the lives of those who accept the saving work of Christ is an essential part of Paul's message (see Rom 6:6), and is so important in Christian theology that no more than a reminder of that can be offered here. Note that here, as elsewhere in Ezekiel, repentance is a result of redemption (vss. 31–32).

The Transformation of Nature

Neither the improvement of the institutions of human society nor the conversion of individuals is enough to produce the world which God wants for us. Both are necessary, but something more is also called for, and this is a change which has largely been ignored in both Jewish and Christian theology. Ezekiel emphasizes it in both chapters 34 and 36, and similar hopes are to be found in the works of other prophets. Nature itself has been corrupted by human sin, the OT claims (see Gen 3:17–18), and is also in need of redemption. Ezekiel promises that transformation of nature will accompany the other changes, for the ideal human life is dependent upon a whole world which is in harmony (see Isa 11:6–9; 35:1–10; 43:20; Hos 2:18, etc.). As in chapter 34 his principal concern is hunger, so the changes which are described have to do for the most part with fertility (vss. 29–30, 34–35), but other OT texts speak of even more striking changes in the natural world. Salvation is a comprehensive act, involving all of God's creation.

Even though the NT generally shows little interest in the natural world, the same, cosmic understanding of redemption does appear a few times, especially in Rom 8:19–23 and Col 1:15–20, and several of the details of the new heaven and new earth promised in the book of Revelation are taken from

Ezekiel (with the expression, "new heaven and new earth" a quotation from Isa 65:17). It must be admitted that in the past the church has found little of value in these materials. It has taken its mission to be the saving of humanity and the provision of food, healing, and peace, as far as that can be done in this life. The natural world has been little more than the stage on which the human drama is acted out, and the reservoir of resources for which to be thankful. But those who now take environmental concerns with the seriousness they deserve may be delighted to discover that the OT has anticipated their convictions and provides texts from which to preach the responsibilities of God's people toward the world which God made and is in the process of redeeming.

Resurrection and Reunion
(Ezekiel 37:1–28)

This chapter contains the classical text on which a theology of exile and restoration may be based. It has been used a great deal in preaching and is a special favorite in the Black churches, where it is perhaps better understood than in most other Christian communions. It is unfortunate, however, that the song, "Dem Bones," has suggested to many people, who know nothing more about Ezekiel than what they have heard in those lyrics, that there is something comic about this chapter, for that is far from the truth. It deals quite literally with a matter of life and death. We must say that the traditional uses of the chapter as it appears in the history of the church, have been slightly off the mark, for it has regularly been taken as a proof-text for the belief in the resurrection of the body in the last days, but that is very clearly not the original intention of the passage. This is a good example of how the interests which one brings to a text tend to determine what one finds there. It has something to say about personal resurrection, certainly, as we shall see, but in emphasizing that the church has missed a more central message, which serves to connect the Testaments theologically. This is a text which proclaims the death and resurrection of God's people, and as such it points directly toward the death and resurrection of Jesus, forcing us to consider why our salvation must be achieved by such drastic means.

In his other oracles of promise Ezekiel has described in some detail the future which he is convinced God is at work to create for his people, and he knows that includes radical changes in the people themselves. He has understood that the ground on which those hopes are based is to be found nowhere in his community, but only in the nature of God himself. Now he finds a vivid way of showing how miraculous that change for the better really is, and he recounts another visionary experience.

Resurrection (37:1–14)

We hear of one more proverb which circulates in the streets of the exilic community. It is clear that the cataclysm of 587 has passed and its meaning has been fully absorbed by those people whom Ezekiel had futilely tried to prepare to accept it. There is no more complacency now, no more insistence on their own righteousness, for those feelings have been replaced by despair. "Our bones are dried up, and our hope is lost; we are clean cut off," he hears them saying. We're dead, the proverb declared; Israel is dead. It seems Ezekiel had heard it so often and brooded on it so long that finally it triggered one of his visionary experiences, for under the impress of the hand of the Lord he found himself out on the flat, alluvial plain of the Tigris-Euphrates river valley, and all around him were scattered bones—disarticulated skeletons, parched white in the sun, as dead as anything could be. "Son of man, can these bones live?" The question he hears would be nonsense in anything other than a vision, but since the prophet knew it was God speaking he gave the right answer: "Lord, you know" (with emphasis on "you" in Hebrew). That was not a refusal to answer, but was truly an expression of the faith of Israel in his day. They believed in a God who gives life and takes it away; who can, if he chooses restore the dead to life (as indicated especially by the stories of resuscitations associated with Elijah and Elisha), so it was a part of Israel's faith to believe that if Yahweh wished to take a pile of bones and bring them to life, he could do so. But Israel in that day would not have answered, "Yes, Lord, I know these bones will live, in the last day, at the resurrection of the dead," to paraphrase Martha's answer to Jesus before the tomb of Lazarus (John 11:24). There is no evidence in the OT prior to the time of Ezekiel of any general expectation of resurrection, so the appropriate answer from a believing Israelite was, "If it is your will, I believe you have the power to make them live," and that is essentially what Ezekiel said.

He is then commanded to prophesy to the bones, again a nonsensical thing outside a vision, and even a very unusual thing for a visionary experience, for Ezekiel not only sees things which are outside the normal realm of human experience, as in chapter 1, but also participates in what is happening in the vision. The message he is commanded to proclaim is strongly reminiscent of the story of how human beings were created, in Gen 2. First God shaped an inanimate figure, then he put breath into it so that it became a living being, and so here Ezekiel's first word produces a plain covered with corpses, and then the second word calls upon the spirit to enter into them, whereupon they all stand up alive.

End of vision. There they stand, whoever they are. All that matters for the point of the vision is that what was once completely and convincingly and apparently permanently dead is now alive—alive because God said, "Live."

Now the vision is interpreted. "Son of man, these bones are the whole house of Israel." The vision has confirmed that for once what the exiles thought and kept saying is right! For once Ezekiel doesn't argue with them, doesn't try to say, "No, no, cheer up; there's still life in our midst." Quite the contrary; in the vision God tells the prophet, "They're right; Israel is dead." Certainly, there are still live people, standing up and walkng around and still complaining, but everything that had once created a people of Yahweh, Israel, is gone.

The question which Ezekiel heard in his vision now takes on new significance: "Son of man, can these bones live?" Is there any imaginable possibility of a future for Israel, for the reappearance on earth of a people of Yahweh? And Ezekiel's answer is even wiser than we first realized, for this has to do with more than resuscitating a human being. We have considered the evidence that Ezekiel realized all was lost, at the human level. But he does not answer God, "Not a chance." He says, "Lord, you know." The future belongs to God, and it will be whatever God determines it shall be.

This chapter begins by telling us that the diagnosis of the situation after 587 is: The patient has died. Then comes the gospel. No obituary here, but page one of a new biography! "Behold, I will open your graves, and raise you from your graves, O my people; and I will bring you home into the land of Israel."

It was mentioned earlier that the church has always wanted this to be a text about the resurrection of individuals in the last day, for the obvious reason that this is an important part of our doctrine. Until recent years, most commentators on the passage have scarcely even mentioned its literal meaning, which is the restoration of Israel to the Promised Land. Among the Church Fathers, Tertullian did acknowledge that this is what it says, but then quickly goes on to what is really important, namely the Christian doctrine of the resurrection of the body. We now ask the question, however, whether the literal meaning may be of importance for us. This is corporate resurrection, the creation of a new people of Yahweh to take the place of that people which had atrophied and died, and it is important to note that "raise you from your graves" is paralleled by "bring you home into the land of Israel." The language of the covenant, which Israel had consistently insisted on breaking and which had finally been abrogated by God, according to the prophets, reappears in this promise, as it did in chapters 34 and 36. Dwelling safely in the land had been the heart of the covenant promise. They had lost the land, but now God says, "I will bring you home." And twice in these few sentences he uses part of the covenant formulary: My people. God announces to those who concluded that all is lost: Now I am ready to start over.

The importance of the exile and restoration for biblical theology has been largely overlooked until very recently. One of the reasons for it has been the traditional Christian desire to find something basically wrong with post-exilic Judaism, in order to reassure ourselves of the superiority of our own faith. So it has been hard for us to consider post-exilic Judaism as a resurrection. Also, the historical materials begin to become fragmentary from this point on, so it has been hard for us to be as clear as we need to be about exactly what happened after the time of Ezekiel. Within recent years, however, a new interest in the exile and restoration has appeared, and the theological potency of this subject is becoming apparent. As one preaches on this text it is important to get the most from it. Is it only a prediction of the death and resurrection of Christ, or did something happen to Israel in those years of exile which can legitimately be called death and resurrection, a true type of the experiences of our Savior? Ezekiel has certainly tried to offer an abundance of evidence to justify saying that Israel died in 587 B.C.; what is more difficult to decide is whether there is anything in Israel's history which can legitimately be called a resurrection. In a few paragraphs, some evidence will be offered to help you make your own decision.

For almost two centuries, prophets had been appearing from time to time to announce that God was about to bring to an end the present order, all that their people had always depended on to keep them safe and secure. It had been announced and explained as judgment, as the justly deserved result of their persistent refusal to uphold their side of the covenant, which the prophets interpreted as outright rebellion. But now Ezekiel has moved beyond that interpretation to show us that the real purpose which God had in mind in bringing all this suffering on his people was not punishment, but to make it possible to create a new people. He acknowledged as his predecessors had done that the conditions for creating a new people had to involve killing the old people first; starting all over. That has happened; now he can promise resurrection. Our question is, was that promise fulfilled, in any meaningful sense, prior to the resurrection of the faithful remnant, Jesus Christ?

Here the book of Ezekiel fails us, for it does not cover time enough after 587 in enough detail to enable us to see the results of his work. Although we have no other records for the exile years to enable us to see what other people or forces may have been active, the results of the exile experience can be documented from later sources. For our purposes, the work of Second Isaiah (Isa 40—55), who addressed the exiles in Babylonia just about a generation after the time of Ezekiel, will provide sufficient evidence that something almost miraculous happened during those undocumented years. The anonymous prophet of the exile does not provide nearly as much evidence about what his (or her) audience believed as Ezekiel does, but the message of Second Isaiah is radically different from every previous prophet in many respects, and it seems fair to conclude that this is not a totally new creation of the mind of this prophet alone, but that it reflects at least in part the faith of the community which is addressed. That is, perhaps we can learn from Isa 40—55 something about how that second generation in exile differed from the people to whom Ezekiel spoke.

(1). In Isa 40—55 explicit monotheism appears for the first time in the Bible. The "practical monotheism" of the first commandment, which informs Israel only that there is but one God with whom they are to have anything to do, is to be found throughout the OT, but Second Isaiah insists there is but one God who exists (see 44:6–8). That this is not just one prophet's idea is indicated by the evidence from this time on that Jews of all kinds have committed themselves to monotheism and are willing to die rather than give it up. Eventually they will die for it.

(2). Idolatry, which had been a perennial threat to the Mosaic religion from the very beginning and had never been conquered, despite the efforts of prophets and reforming kings, and which still remained a threat to the exilic community, as we have seen in Ezekiel, is for Second Isaiah just something to make fun of. The very idea that the true God can be represented by anything in the created world has now become so out of the question for the Jews that they simply caricature the use of idols, as in Isa 44:9–20. Everything that is was made by God, but God is separate from it all and different from everything in the natural world (Isa 40:12, 18, 22; 45:18).

(3). Second Isaiah finds no need to criticize his or her audience for injustice or inequalities within their community. That major element of the message of all the prophets from Amos through Ezekiel is missing from this prophet's work. What has happened? The evidence we have says that these people finally have changed. Sometimes this prophet does scold, rather than announcing judgment, and that is new. He scolds them for being discouraged, for finding it hard to believe the message that restoration is now at hand. They have not been used to hearing good news, and that is the main fault which Second Isaiah finds with them. They are not criticized for putting their confidence in the wrong things, as Ezekiel did; neither are they condemned for refusing to take the will of God for their lives seriously. They have changed.

But had they changed radically enough that we may be justified, theologically, in calling it a resurrection, the fulfillment of Ezekiel's promise? He had been vague about *when* all the good things in chapters 34, 36, and 37 would happen, but a generation later Second Isaiah said it's beginning to happen now. To the appearance of Cyrus the Great in the Middle East this prophet tied the restoration of the diaspora and the rebuilding and glorification of Zion, with the blossoming of the wilderness to accompany it. Now we must once again ask the question which those who followed Second Isaiah must also have asked. Did it happen? Or was Second Isaiah wrong?

The soundest answer seems to be that he was partly right. In the restoration which began shortly after 538 B.C. those promises *began* to be fulfilled. Shortly after those extravagant words were written, Cyrus did make it possible for exiled Jews to return to their homeland, some of them did go back, and within a few years a temple was rebuilt and the worship of Yahweh in Jerusalem was resumed. The wilderness did not bloom and Zion did not become the glory of all the earth, but even so, at the beginning of the restoration period the prophets Haggai and Zechariah did insist that what was happening should be understood as fulfillment (Zech 7–8).

Resurrection may not be too strong a word for it. Consider again what happened to Judah. In 587 B.C., Judah died. It was not a very big event in the history of the time. How many Middle Eastern nations and city-states have risen, flourished, and died in the past 4000 years, or more? No one knows how many, but we can list the names and fates of dozens. And for all those nations but one, it was simply the end. But one nation—a small one, a weak one, a poor one—lost everything like the others, was scattered among the great nations of the East, but somehow did not lose its identity.

No longer was it a nation, with its own land, government, or even its own language. But it existed as a people, defined by a unique religion; it was a congregation. Only God knows how that could have happened, but from the human perspective we must say it was in part because the survivors of that cataclysm remembered, accepted, and acted upon the prophets' interpretation of what was *really* happening, what God was up to, in that one particular invasion, amid *those* burning cities, dying people, strangers and exiles wandering the earth—on the surface of it just another catastrophe like hundreds of others. But those prophetic words of judgment and now of promise told the survivors that this time something unique was happening, a mighty redeeming act of God.

Something unique did happen. The exile and restoration were the death and resurrection of a people in history, as close to a documentable miracle as we shall probably ever find. The exile foreshadows the cross in that both of them reveal to us

how desperate is our need, how futile and feeble our efforts to
obey, and how perennial our rebellion. The restoration foreshadows the resurrection of Christ; both of them miraculous
acts of God for our redemption, creating new life where there
had been only defeat and death. And that is not the end of the
pattern, the NT tells us. Paul wrote, "But if we have died with
Christ, we believe that we shall also live with him" (Rom 6:8),
and the whole story, from Israel to Paul, may just be enough to
convince us that we are by nature neither better nor worse than
Ezekiel's congregation, so that for us also the message of our
own death and resurrection is gospel.

Reunion (37:15–28)

This passage is a logical addition to the promise of resurrection. The offer of new life to the exiles left one great scandal still unresolved. They were Judeans, but the people of
God had originally comprised the descendants of the twelve
sons of Jacob, and there were two calamities in the past
about which Ezekiel felt the need to speak. He had already
incorporated the fall of the Northern Kingdom and the exile
of the ten tribes into his own experiences of judgment, in the
symbolic act of lying for 390 days on his left side (4:4–8),
showing his concern for an event which had occurred long
before, in 722 B.C. But the end of the political existence of the
Northern Kingdom was not the only calamity. Two hundred
years before that, the short-lived unity of the twelve tribes,
which had been accomplished by David and preserved by
Solomon, had been sundered when Solomon's son Reho-
boam came to the throne (1 Kings 12). As Ezekiel considered
God's intentions for his people he came to the conviction that
resurrected Israel would not be confined to the survivors of
597 and 587, to only those exiled from Judah and Jerusalem,
but concluded that all Israel must be involved.

In a very simple symbolic act, Ezekiel announced to the
exiles that it was God's plan to bring together all the twelve
tribes from wherever they may have been exiled, restore
them to the Promised Land and give them one king, as in the
time of David. He expresses a hope which can also be found
in Jeremiah's work (3:6—4:2; 31:1–22). Several of the
promises which appeared in chapters 34 and 36 are now repeated against the background of the message that Israel will

be reunited: the righteous king (David), the ability to obey, the repossession of the land, the establishment of a covenant of peace, and the witness of the nations. One new element appears, which will be developed at great length in chapters 40—48, and that is the promise that God will set his sanctuary in their midst for evermore. The equivalent to that promise, that God would dwell in their midst, has appeared before, but ordinarily Ezekiel avoids using the word "sanctuary" in a positive sense, obviously because of his conviction that the sanctuary he knew had been hopelessly defiled.

A new temple was built by returned Judeans, but the essence of this promise has never been fulfilled. It must be emphasized that most of what has been said about the "Ten Lost Tribes of Israel" is fiction, for they really were not lost at all. There are fragments of evidence from the Assyrian period and later which enable us to document the continuing existence of the descendants of those who were exiled from the Northern Kingdom into North Mesopotamia. In the Apocrypha, the book of Tobit contains a legend about a family of faithful Yahwists from the tribe of Naphtali who are living in exile in Assyria. This story was written and preserved by Jews, but it seems very unlikely that it is complete fiction. It probably reflects some of their continuing knowledge of the lives of the remnants of the Northern Kingdom. In the later rabbinic literature there is an account of the journey of a rabbi from Palestine to North Mesopotamia to visit exiles from the Ten Tribes, and this account is accompanied by a discussion of when the Twelve Tribes will once again be reunited.

For Christians, this reminds us of a sensitive subject, the occurrence and aftereffects of schism in the church. We have a painful history of disunity, and must also confess that Jesus' prayer, as recorded in John 17, "that they may all be one" (vs. 21), has by no means yet been fulfilled. But the prophets and Jesus agree that divisions among the people of God are a scandal and that God's intention for us is to make us one (Eph 2:14–16). Any preaching from texts such as this one, then, should very properly emphasize nonfulfillment, and should put the challenge before us, asking what we can begin to do to overcome the ancient and lasting scandal of schism.

Gog
(Ezekiel 38:1—39:29)

The book of Ezekiel might have come to a very satisfying conclusion with chapter 37, or one might have moved from 37 to chapters 40—48, feeling that the transition from the promise of a sanctuary in their midst, in 37:26–28, to the extensive description of the new temple in 40—48 was fully appropriate. But instead the reader is surprised by a new and completely unexpected act in the great drama of the future, the story of the futile attack of a coalition of northern peoples against the Holy Land. This unit fits the rest of Ezekiel's message so poorly and is so different from his style and main interests that many scholars think most or all of it is the work of his disciples, who set about to apply his teachings to a new situation. That is a critical conclusion concerning date and authorship which has a great deal in its favor, but we in the church have inherited the book with those chapters included and we do not preach from some hypothetical, original Ezekiel (the text of which would vary from scholar to scholar), but from the canonical book which the believing community has confessed to be the word of God from century to century. So we do not worry so much about whether Ezekiel really wrote this, but ask instead what these chapters have said to the believing community as they have found them within Ezekiel's book. The fact is that they have had a profound influence on the development of apocalyptic thought, and since our own age is one which is filled with apocalyptic hopes and fears, we dare not overlook this passage, even though it may create many difficulties for us. Some of the wrong turns which have been made in the interpretation of these chapters must be disposed of first before considering what they really say and why they are important.

What It Doesn't Mean

Gog is a thoroughly mysterious figure and mystery always breeds speculation. Some parishioners will be much too interested in these chapters and in those flourishing theories which purport to explain everything in terms of current events. Since those theories are typically pronounced with a firm air of certainty, it is important for the interpreter of the passage to know why it actually does *not* mean that.

Where Ezekiel got the name Gog remains unknown. There is no record of any historical figure from his time who bears such a name; neither was there an invasion from the north, or threat of invasion which might have led to this prophecy. This makes the passage very different from the rest of the book, which speaks throughout of known historical characters and events. It is true that the other proper names in chapters 38—39 can be identified, but they are all at the fringes of the known world and play no role in the history Ezekiel records.

The best guess so far, and it is only a guess, is that here the prophet once again borrows from the lore of the Middle East, as he did in using the myth of the cosmic tree and in alluding to the legendary king Daniel, and is making creative use of a story (otherwise unknown to us) about an earlier king of Lydia (part of Asia Minor) whose name was Gugu (known as Gyges to Greek writers). Put into Hebrew this name would come out Gug or Gog. As a historical character he does not explain anything in chapters 38—39, but if he was remembered in Ezekiel's time as a mysterious, legendary figure from the threatening north, it would account for the choice of the name to denote the great prince of the future.

Many suggestions have been made which do not look for some figure in Ezekiel's past or present as the basis for Gog, but which consider the name to be a cipher for some figure in his future. One study lists thirteen different identifications, including Alexander the Great and the Antichrist. It is the latter type of approach, which tends to think that the true Gog has just recently appeared in history, which attracts people, despite the absence of solid evidence showing the chapter should be read that way.

In this century, it is the word Rosh which has attracted special attention, for obvious reasons. He is called "Gog, prince of Rosh, Meshech and Tubal." No place named Rosh is known from ancient documents, and since the Hebrew word means "head, chief, first" many translators have as-

sumed that the grammar is a bit irregular here, and have
rendered the expression "Gog, chief prince of Meshech and
Tubal." But there is an old tradition which has associated
Rosh with Russia. There are only two reasons for this: (1)
The words sound somewhat alike. (2) The coalition is said to
come from the "the uttermost parts of the north" (38:6). For
people who do not insist on historical evidence to back up
their theories, that seems to be proof enough. They will then
go on to identify Meshech with Moscow and Tubal with
Tobalsk, simply because they are vaguely similar. But
Meshech and Tubal are no mysteries; they are known from
other ancient documents as well as the OT to be places in
eastern Asia Minor (see also Gen 10:2), so their identification
with modern cities is nonsense. As for Russia, the earliest evidence for the place name is fom the ninth century A.D., when
a tribe on the river Dnieper was called Ros or Rus, and we
have no trace of any group or place bearing a name like this
for the 1400 years or so between that time and Ezekiel's date.
Of course, there is a certain theory of inspiration which
would say that has nothing to do with it, for Ezekiel was not
talking about anything in his own day, he was talking about
twentieth-century Russia and nothing else. This leaves some
serious questions unanswered, however. If Rosh was a completely meaningless place-name in his day, and Meshech did
not mean the Meshech of his time but the future city of Moscow, then would that not make his words completely meaningless to his own people, and worse than meaningless—
misleading? And if it be claimed that God really did see fit to
have something recorded in writing in the sixth century B.C.
which no one could understand until the twentieth century
A.D., why didn't he spell it our way? Why Rosh, if he really
wrote it for us? Every other name in the passage has to do
with peoples or places known to have existed in antiquity,
and if Rosh is really a name, and not just the word meaning
"chief," then the best we can do is say it is as yet unidenti-
fied, and there is no evidence to connect it with the later
name of Russia.

What It Says

It is difficult to ascertain any clear, logical progression of
thought through these two chapters. In chapter 38, Gog is

called by Yahweh to gather the armies of the north to march against Palestine, and they are destroyed by a great earthquake. Then the commissioning is repeated at the beginning of chapter 39 and their destruction briefly recorded, followed by a lengthy description of the process of burial. After that the birds and beasts are called to come to eat the flesh of the dead soldiers, who should have all been buried by then, if things were in chronological order. Finally, 39:21–29 makes no explicit reference at all to the preceding verses, and reminds us very much of concluding statements to other chapters such as 16:59–64; 20:42–44; 37:25–28. It contains a theology which has been discussed earlier; that redemption is the cause rather than the result of significant changes in human attitudes.

We seem to have a collection of loosely organized paragraphs concerning Gog, and many scholars think that the core of it may be 39:1–8, which has then been elaborated in various, not very well-connected ways. But the intention of the whole collection is clear. This is a message of assurance that the day is coming when the power of Yahweh will be made known to the whole world, or as Ezekiel puts it, when he will vindicate his holiness before the eyes of the nations (38:16). It takes up a theological question which is not so directly relevant to the needs of the exiles as the other questions which have been dealt with in the book. Its "distance" is made clear by the temporal terms which are used: "after many days" (38:8), "on that day" (38:10), "in the latter days" (38:16). Everything else in the book has been addressed to someone's immediate needs, but this is different. It is set in some future time after the restoration has occurred (38:8, 11–12, 14), when presumably all that had been promised in chapters 34; 36—37 had been fulfilled. These chapters contain an advance warning that new dangers will arise, even in those times of blessings, and they refer to earlier prophets, whose predictions were not considered to have been fulfilled (38:17). This is probably a reference to the warnings of the enemy from the north in Jeremiah (see 4:6). It should also be noted that the apparent contradiction between 38:3–9 and 10–16, in which God first sends Gog against Palestine, then condemns him for his own intentions is probably also based on an earlier passage, in which Isaiah is a bit clearer about the distinction

between God's use of a great nation as an agent of judgment
and the greed and self-esteem of the nation itself, which also
leaves it subject to eventual judgment. That makes much better sense in Isa 10:5–19 than it does here, where no reason for
judgment of the chosen people is given. The subject is really
entirely different, even though the development of it has been
influenced by several earlier prophecies. It takes the old, cultic
theme of the rebellion of nations against the Lord's anointed
and his chosen city, such as we find reflected in Pss 2; 46; 48;
and 76 and projects it into the future as a way of affirming the
literal, historical validity of what the cult had always proclaimed to be true: that Yahweh is king over all the nations.

This addition to traditional OT eschatology, of another act
beyond the restoration, in which the Holy Land is threatened
by a terrifying coalition of nations, only to have God himself
intervene to destroy them all and end the threat forever, has
had a continuing influence. The same theme is elaborated in
Zech 12 and 14, and then it reappears in Jewish apocalyptic as
a standard feature of depictions of the Last Judgment. Jesus'
predictions of the fall of Jerusalem (Mark 13 and parallels)
stand in this tradition and of course Rev 20:7–10 makes its de-
pendence explicit by referring to Gog and Magog by name.
Lengthy studies of the theme have been made, but cannot even
be summarized here. As we consider what may be preachable
in these chapters, to ask the question *why* these ideas became
so popular and have enjoyed periodic revivals of popularity up
to this very day may lead us to some useful conclusions.

What It Means

It was mentioned earlier that this cannot be understood as
a message concerning any immediate need of Jews in exile,
but when we begin to consider the actual conditions of life in
the Judean community after the restoration began, we can
see some relevance which is otherwise missing. The new
community, settled around the rebuilt temple, had to face up
to the fact that restoration was incomplete and that new dangers continued to arise. (See especially the evidence for the
fifth century in the book of Nehemiah.) The new and unexpected stage in the prophetic depiction of the future which is
announced in chapters 38—39 now makes allowances for
new outbreaks of trouble, even after God's promises have be-

gun to be fulfilled. For a people, i.e., post-exilic Judaism, whose lives in many ways were the proof that the experience of exile truly had brought in a new age of faithfulness, but who found that to be faithful could lead to agonizing suffering instead of peace and prosperity, it was essential to believe that there was at least one more round in the fight against evil. The rise of apocalyptic literature represented one effort to provide a justification for the suffering of the righteous, by assuring them that, in effect this new calamity which had just befallen them was the fulfillment of the prophecy concerning Gog, whose doom was sure.

Such apocalyptic moments have continued to recur in history. Believers who have been enjoying a reasonable measure of security suddenly find themselves threatened by terrifying forces which jeopardize prosperity sometimes and at other times safety and life itself. That is to say, from time to time, and not least in our own time, believers find themselves confronting Gog again, and they need that same reassurance which is proclaimed by Ezek 38—39: No matter what the threat may be, no matter how immense or how grotesque, God is still in charge.

Someone said about the Aleutian Islands, "They're not the end of the world, but you can see it from there." Something very much like that can be said for the many desperate situations which believers have faced and survived, since Ezekiel's time. No one of them was the end of the world, after all, but at the time they could see the end from there, and the message they needed just then was a message for those who face the end. Historical disasters, personal calamities, which to the onlooker seem no different from what many others have endured, may to the participant take on apocalyptic dimensions, and for them it is a blessing that an apocalyptic assurance is available. There is nothing in these chapters with which to calculate and it simply must be said that those who use them to gauge the signs of the times, to estimate how much longer it will be before the Second Coming, have misunderstood them. These chapters are for those people who have faced and for those people who will face a threat which takes on the existential dimensions of Gog and his hordes, and the message of these chapters to them is to be found in 39:7—8.

The New Jerusalem
(Ezekiel 40:1—48:35)

We are used to visions by now, but this one is very different. Aspects of it show a close relationship with the rest of the book, especially the reappearance of the throne chariot in 43:1–9, but in much of it the visionary qualities disappear completely and it sounds more like an excerpt from Leviticus or Numbers than like the work of a prophet. Although it is introduced the same way the other visions in the book are introduced, it is very long (nine chapters) and we never come to a conclusion approaching anything like what is found in chapters 3; 11; or 37. No interpretation of its meaning is provided and there is no indication of how the vision is to affect Ezekiel or his community. This presents a very difficult problem to the interpreter. Is it essentially present tense, like chapters 1—3, partly present and partly future, like 8—11, or future, like 37? That may seem a stupid question to ask when every commentary labels this section "The Vision of the New Temple," or something similar, but note that the passage does not explicitly say anything futuristic. There is no "in that day," or "days are coming," no "Behold, I will...." Ezekiel sees it all before him "in visions of God" (40:2), and is told to describe the temple to the house of Israel, "that they may be ashamed of their iniquities" (40:4; 43:10). But in addition to what he sees there are lengthy passages of what he hears; laws of holiness for this sanctuary and plans for the division of the Holy Land. Many scholars think the visionary parts, proper, may be the work of Ezekiel himself and they ascribe the legal materials to priests whose interest in a new temple drew them to add their own contributions to Ezekiel's picture. Others deny that the prophet had anything to do with these chapters and only a few try to explain everything in them as the work of Ezekiel. Since early times the legal materials have been a problem, since they do not agree in all respects with the laws of the Pentateuch, so the early rabbis struggled to harmonize the two. We cannot devote much space to the legal material, but it cannot be ignored completely, for there is a single concern which runs through these chapters, unifying them, and we shall confine our thoughts at this point to the way the laws reflect that concern.

It is hard to imagine reading in worship very many of the paragraphs in this section as a text from which to preach. Even the translation of much of it is very uncertain and passages such as chapters 40—42 make for dull reading. There are some potentially valuable texts, however, especially 47:1–12, and the discussion which follows will point them out, while attempting to explain their context by means of an exposition of the central theological theme of these chapters.

Several very different efforts have been made to interpret chapters 40—48, and three of them will be described briefly before the theology of the section is presented. (1). They have been taken as a literal building plan to be followed by those who would one day return from exile and rebuild the temple. The detailed regulations for worship in the visionary temple fit this interpretation very neatly, and the presence of elements which no human being could contrive, such as its location on a very high mountain (40:2) and the miraculous stream of water which the prophet saw flowing from under its threshold (47:1) are not strong arguments against it, since later prophets believed that once the people began to build, God would also take a hand (Hag 2; Zech 8). The concept of a visionary seeing the heavenly plan for a structure which human beings were to build was a familiar one in the ancient Near East, as the inscriptions of the Sumerian King Gudea show, and it appears in the OT in the accounts of how the tabernacle was built (compare Exod 25—31 with 35—40). But if that was the intention of this passage it was something of a failure, for neither Zerubbabel's temple nor Herod the Great's reconstruction of it followed Ezekiel's plan. Apparently the returnees did not read these chapters this way.

(2). Various kinds of futuristic interpretations, including especially dispensationalism, take this to be a still completely unfulfilled prophecy, which will literally come true in the Last Days. Of course, no one can say for certain what will or will not happen in the Last Days, but this way of reading the section does not fit at all well with traditional Christian theology, since it involves believing that the entire sacrificial system will once again be reestablished. Most Christians do not seem to believe that is either meaningful or acceptable, in the light of what the NT says about sacrifice. And since the passage does not represent itself explicitly as a prediction, it need not be read that way.

(3). The interpretation which will be offered here understands these chapters to be "theology in visual terms." As Ezekiel elsewhere expressed his message via allegory, symbolic acts, and the accounts of visionary experiences, and as apocalyptic later used extensive and complex symbolism to work through the theological problems which concerned it, so these chapters can be seen to make use of a variety of ways of expressing a single theme.

There are two texts which show us explicitly what chapters 40—48 are all about. Once they are recognized, then it becomes clear that everything else in the section is a development of the same theme. The first is 43:1–9, in which Ezekiel sees the glory of Yahweh return to Jerusalem, accompanied by the promise, "and I will dwell in their midst for ever." The second puts it in another way. It is the last verse of the book, "And the name of the city henceforth shall be, 'Yahweh is there'" (48:35). This is a response to the exiles' deepest need, to be sure that God is with them. Since most of us can identify with that same need, we begin to read these chapters with more interest. They speak in four quite different ways of the assurance that Yahweh intends to dwell in the midst of his people, and it seems that the clearest way to present them will be to organize the materials under those four headings.

Visions of God (40:1–2a; 43:1–9; 44:4)

Once again, in a vision, Ezekiel is taken to Jerusalem, nineteen years after that visionary journey in which he had seen the extent of the corruption which affected the sanctuary itself and witnessed the departure of the glory of the Lord from the city (chaps. 8—11). But this is a different Jerusalem. There seem to be no people there except the prophet and his supernatural guide and he witnesses only one event. That event is of great significance, however, for it is the return of the throne chariot to the temple (43:1–9). This would certainly be a preachable text if one were doing a short series of sermons from Ezekiel, for it adds a final word of explanation of the significance of the appearances of God to this prophet. There were three. In the first, the man who had been carried far from the Holy Land encountered his God in an alien place—living, active, and present. Not long after that he saw Jerusalem in a vision, and there in Jerusalem was the same throne chariot—leaving. As a part of his interpretation of the meaning of that experience he spoke of the implications of his earlier encounter with God in Babylonia. Yahweh has been accessible there, has been a sanctuary to the exiles, he affirmed (11:16). That never satisfied them, however, and their hopes remained fixed on Jerusalem even after it was destroyed. Late in his life, Ezekiel saw a confirmation of those hopes; no people yet, but a city and a land ready for them and the real presence of God there in its midst. This is the confirmation of our conclusions about what God was doing in all the sorrowful events of these years. The goal of them all was not to destroy or to punish or to reject or to humiliate, but to make it possible to have a perfect city where an obedient people could live with God in their midst. The author of Revelation understood the central theme of these chapters very well indeed, and as he spoke of God's intent for us in chapters 21 and 22, could find no better way to do so than to describe again Ezekiel's new Jerusalem.

Transformation of Myth (40:2; 47:1–12)

We have seen abundant evidence of the combination of learning and creativity in Ezekiel's allegories. Once again he draws from the mythological materials familiar to the people of the ancient Near East in order to express an important message about God's intention. He makes only a brief allusion to the one idea, but develops the other one lovingly. The whole vision, it seems from 40:2, is set on a very high mountain. Now, Mt. Zion is not even as high as the hills around it, but we have no doubt that is where Ezekiel finds himself. This is simply a brief allusion to the concept of the "world mountain," of which more is made in Isa 2:2–4 (Mic 4:1–4) and Zech 14:10. The city of God is theologically (not geologically) the highest point on earth because that claim would remind people of myths of the world mountain, which con-

nected heaven and earth. What it was really saying was: You
can have access to heaven there. You can find God there. So
the reference to the very high mountain is just one more,
very brief allusion to that same theme which we are finding
expressed in a variety of ways in this section.

In 47:1–12, the concept of the water of life, which also appears in myth, is tied to Jerusalem. Because God is there, the
temple becomes a spring of life, welling up and spreading beyond the sanctuary. The blessings of God's presence in the
city cannot be confined to that one place, and that is nowhere depicted more effectively than in this detailed description of how the water courses down through the desolation of
the Wilderness of Judea to the Dead Sea, making everything
alive and fertile as it goes.

This is a text which can and should be preached. It is one
of the best examples of the way the OT combines its concerns
for the redemption of nature with its central concern for full
and rich human life on earth. Where God is present, the desert blooms. This is the classical example of the truth God
brings life out of death, expressed in terms of the natural
world, as the author of Revelation recognized. He quotes this
passage, condensing and rewriting it somewhat, and speaks
of the river of the water of life (Rev 22:1–2). He leaves out the
transformation of the Dead Sea, but may refer to it when he
adds, "There shall no more be anything accursed" (22:3). In
Ezekiel, the brine of the Dead Sea miraculously becomes
fresh water brimming with fish when it is touched by the
water of life originating in the temple. So just as the curse
brought on nature by human sin rebounds against people
(Gen 3:17–19 and see Lev 26:34–35, 43; Deut 28:23–24), now
the transformation of nature results in abundance for people.
The fish are there to be caught and eaten (vs. 10). But the
prophet remembered that the Dead Sea does have one value
for people as it is, for it is a source of salt, and so his vision
does not depict a new age which will bring deprivation in
any way. It makes provisions for the salt still to be there, in
the marshes, because people need it. The trees along the
stream are also there not just for their own sakes, but to provide fruit for food and leaves for healing.

Many centuries after these words were written the curse on
nature still prevails, and our worst industrial and urban

areas are the proof of it. We have created new wastelands. But this text should not be dismissed thereby as mere daydreaming, or interpreted as merely symbolic of God's spiritual blessings. We ought to take this as a clear statement of what God wants for us and his world. We may find it hard to see any evidence of the beginnings of God's transformation of nature, and yet the gospel says we do not have to wait until the eschaton without any foretaste of redemption. The fullness of God's redemptive work began to come true in Jesus Christ, we are taught and believe. Does that apply in any way to this text?

We may begin with the concluding statement, that the leaves of the trees will be for healing, and remind ourselves that Jesus accepted the role of healer as a major part of his ministry. The early church understood the significance of that, and also took healing, both physical and spiritual, to be the central part of its task on earth. Feeding the hungry was another of the signs Jesus performed as a way of showing that the Kingdom of God was at hand, and the church has recognized that it has the privilege of providing signs of the presence of the Kingdom on earth as it also feeds the hungry. If these things are true, and it does not seem likely that there will be much debate over them, then why cannot we also add that everything we do to make deserts blossom is in accord with what God is doing as he works toward the culmination of his will for us.

It has not happened yet in the Wilderness of Judea, but wherever there is healing and blossoming and food for the hungry it is a sign that the blessings Ezekiel saw flowing from Jerusalem are coming true. They are evidence that God is there.

The Center (40:3—42:20; 45:1-8; 47:13—48:35)

This body of material is very different from anything else to be found in the prophetic books. It reminds us of the descriptions of the tabernacle and of Solomon's temple, but even differs from them in significant respects. The passages which describe how the land is to be divided among the tribes are reminiscent of Josh 13—21, but that earlier plan followed the landmarks of the country, and this one just draws straight lines east to west across the land. All the

commentators remark on the unrealistic nature of such a
plan, for a hilly country, and some have also claimed that if
the tribes were given equal amounts of land the Holy City
would be located at Mt. Gerizim, not Mt. Zion, a highly dis-
turbing result for a Jewish book! The plan for the temple is
also highly abstract, largely because it is essentially just a
ground plan. Except for the descriptions of the altar
(43:13–17), the rooms alongside the temple (41:5–11;
42:1–14), and the decorations with cherubim and palm
trees there is scarcely any indication what the structures
were intended to look like.

It will be suggested here that this is not a flaw in the writing, but is in perfect accord with the purpose of the material.
The description of the temple provides a ground plan only,
and the allotments for the city, the priests, Levites and tribes
are schematic because the point of this all is to emphasize
the centrality of the holy place, and to provide for the preservation of that holiness.

Recent studies in the History of Religions have shown how
important it was to the archaic mind to have a holy place at
the center of one's life, around which all of one's experiences
could be organized. As a member of a priestly family Ezekiel
had grown up with the tradition of commitment to the preservation of such a holy place, so it is conceivable that at least
some of this material did come from him. Here the priestly
orientation provides another way of developing the assurance of the continuing presence of Yahweh with his people.
The reason the ground plan of the temple is described so
carefully and the rest largely ignored is that its symmetry
emphasizes the centrality of the temple, to which the glory of
the Lord returns.

Then a similar thing is done with the division of the land.
Jerusalem is actually rather far south in Palestine, and in the
original settlement of the land only Judah and Simeon were
located to the south of it. This won't do, however, for the purposes of this idealization, so the historical location of the
tribes is largely ignored. The actual space available is also
unimportant for the most part, to this author, except for one
indication of his knowledge of geography; only five tribes are
located south of Jerusalem and seven to the north, instead of
making it an exactly even division. Still the intention is

clear, to make Jerusalem the center of the country—ideally—even though that was impossible in practice.

The second feature of the division was provision of space for the prince and his family, for priests and Levites, and for locating the temple outside the city, in the priests' portion. This was to preserve its holiness so that it might never again be defiled, for to a priest defilement would mean incurring the danger of Yahweh leaving that place again. But given this rigidly structured system, with such careful provisions for the protection of holy places and things, it is quite remarkable that aliens are to be permitted to settle and to own property in the Holy Land (47:22–23). This stands in some contrast to the strict prohibition of participation of aliens in the temple service, in 44:7–9. The priestly concern for avoiding any potential violation of the holiness of that place appears in that regulation, but it is important to note that 47:22–23 reveals no concept of racial purity is associated with life in the Promised Land.

These passages offer a way of picturing the well-structured life of God's people, oriented around a center from which all blessings flow, and with some provisions for assuring the continuation of those blessings. The fourth way of expressing the promise of God's presence is another priestly effort to preserve and protect it by regulating the behavior of those who come to the center.

The Preservation of Holiness
(43:10–44:3; 44:5–31; 45:9–25)

These materials are unusual only by virtue of their location in the Bible. They are laws for the sanctuary, of the same type which appear in the Pentateuch, and this makes Ezekiel the only lawgiver except Moses in the OT. The problems this created for the rabbis have been mentioned earlier; the problem of ritual law for Christians is admittedly too large to be taken up in this place. Discussion of the details of these regulations seems inappropriate here, and so the only comments which will be offered have to do with the way they fit the comprehensive theme of chapters 40—48.

The vision of what God plans for his people is interrupted by these materials, which are in a different form—legal—and which specify what the people are to do in that new setting.

Given the priestly orientation of the material, the rules all make sense, for they concentrate on what people must do to preserve the holiness of the new Jerusalem. Holiness and the immediate presence of God were inseparable, and the priestly mind now turns from what God does to what people must do. Human responsibility is not forgotten, and certainly the ethical side of that, which is ordinarily so prominent in the prophetic books, is not being challenged by this material (see 45:9–12), even though it is largely missing. But the subject is the temple as the sign of God's presence, and so the ritual laws associated with the temple have naturally come to the fore (43:10–12). The most important thing for us to observe as we read this material is the insistence that in the ideal world, which is God's making, human responsibility for the preservation of that world in its rightness is still essential.

"The Lord Is There" (48:35)

"Where is your God?" was the mocking question which had been asked more than once of suffering Israel (see Pss 79:9–10; 115:1–3). The same question was asked by Israelites of their own God, sometimes as an expression of doubt ("Where is the God of justice?"; Mal 2:17), and at other times as faith's challenge to God to be what he is believed to be (see 2 Kings 2:14; Isa 63: 11–15; Jer 2:6–8). Many times in the Bible God's answer to other questions has taken the form of an answer to this question; his answer to many questions is the assurance, "I am with you," or the promise, "I will be with you." It has been argued that the need to know that God is near has governed the selection of all the materials in chapters 40—48 and that they represent a variety of ways of promising a life with God at the center. The last verse of the book repeats that promise in plain words; the very name of that new city will say it: "The Lord is there."

Surely the need which is addressed here is present among human beings in every generation. The materials chosen to speak to it in the sixth century B.C.—visions, myths and laws of holiness—were no doubt effective then, but the natural ways we would choose to talk about the same subject are usually quite different. Ezekiel's language gets the point across, however; we understand the promise offered here and we know that we need it.

The NT takes up the OT's tendency to connect Jerusalem with the assurance that God is with us and does not reject it completely, even though its central message is that the promise became incarnate in Jesus. As we have seen, Revelation re-projects it into the future, in chapters 21—22, but Hebrews does something even more interesting with it.

> But you have come to Mount Zion and to the city of the living God, the heavenly Jerusalem, and to innumerable angels in festal gathering, and to the assembly of the first-born who are enrolled in heaven, and to a judge who is God of all, and to the spirits of just men made perfect, and to Jesus, the mediator of a new covenant, and to the sprinkled blood that speaks more graciously than the blood of Abel. (Heb 12:22–24)

Hebrews says that already, in the experience of Christian worship, Christians have access to the new Jerusalem. This is the resolution of the tension which we have found in Ezekiel. The Jews discovered and experienced a truth that God is accessible anywhere. Christianity took that truth and found a theology for it. There is an interesting intermediate step in Rev 3:12, where God, Christ, and the New Jerusalem are associated, but Hebrews carries the implications of Incarnation theology to their conclusion and offers its own kind of Amen to the final verse of Ezekiel: Wherever the Spirit brings the presence of the Living Christ we are in the New Jerusalem, for the Lord is there.

Bibliography

We are well supplied with recent commentaries on Ezekiel, ranging from highly technical works to a book prepared for daily Bible study. The most thorough, including text and form criticism, detailed exegesis and theology, is the two-volume work by Walther Zimmerli, *Ezekiel* ("Hermeneia"; Fortress, 1979, 1983). Most useful for the preacher because of its excellent theological insights is Walther Eichrodt, *Ezekiel* ("Old Testament Library"; Westminster, 1970). Briefer, with less theological content, is John W. Wevers, *Ezekiel* ("The New Century Bible Commentary"; Eerdmans, 1969). One volume of a projected two-volume work was available at the time this book was written: Moshe Greenberg, *Ezekiel 1—20* ("Anchor Bible"; Doubleday, 1983).

Recent, brief commentaries: Keith W. Carley, *The Book of the Prophet Ezekiel* ("The Cambridge Bible Commentary"; Cambridge University Press, 1974). Peter C. Craigie, *Ezekiel* ("Daily Study Bible Series"; Westminster, 1983). John B. Taylor, *Ezekiel* ("Tyndale Old Testament Commentaries"; Inter-Varsity Press, 1969).

For background to the approach to preaching from Ezekiel which is represented here, it may be helpful to consult my book, *Reclaiming the Old Testament for the Christian Pulpit* (John Knox, 1980), Chapter 6: "Preaching from the Prophets."